£10 95 6

D0295732

171639

The
CALL OF DUTY

POLICE GALLANTRY IN DEVON & CORNWALL

*Decorations, Orders, Medals and Commendations for Gallantry
and Devotion to Duty awarded to Officers who have served
in the Police Forces of Devon and Cornwall*

ROGER CAMPION

HALSGROVE
In assocation with the Devon & Cornwall Constabulary

First published in Great Britain in 1997

Copyright © 1997, Roger Campion and the Devon & Cornwall Constabulary

*All rights reserved. No part of this publication may be
reproduced, stored in a retrieval system, or copied in any form
or by any means without the prior permission of the copyright holder.*

British Library Cataloguing in Publication Data

CIP record for this book is available from the British Library

ISBN 1 874448 361

HALSGROVE
Halsgrove House
Lower Moor Way
Tiverton
Devon EX16 6SS
Tel: 01884 243242
Fax: 01884 243325

The Call of Duty is published by Halsgrove in association with the
Devon & Cornwall Constabulary.

363.2/cam.

Printed in Great Britain by Bookcraft Ltd, Midsomer Norton

CONTENTS

PICTURE CREDITS

Token Publishing Ltd, Honiton: photos of medals on pages 9, 10, 11, 23, 45, 83, 85, 89, 90, 91, 105, 106, 107, 124

Commonwealth War Graves Commission: photos on pages 77, 80, 81, 128

Tank Museum, Bovington, Dorset: two photos on page 94

Mirror Group Newspapers: page 46

Jim Wright and the 166 Squadron Association: page 89

Albert Labbett, Crediton: page 39

St Ives Museum, Cornwall: three photos on pages 54 and 55

Express and Echo, Exeter: photos on pages 13, 14, 18, 40, 63, 66, 72, 73

Toye, Kenning and Spencer, Manufacturer of medal ribbons: colour photos of OBE, MBE, DSO and MC

Regimental badges and squadron crests are Crown Copyright and reproduced by courtesy of the Ministry of Defence.

Medal ribbons (colour section) were taken from *Medals and Ribbons* by H Taprell, Dorling, published by George Philip and Son Ltd and reprinted by permission of Reed Consumer Books

Imperial War Museum: page 79 (IWM Q6236), p82 (IVM Q 568), p87 (IWM Q5935), p88 (IWM F(AUS)719)

London Gazette citations are Crown Copyright and reproduced with the permission of the Controller of Her Majesty's Stationery Office: pages 15, 36, 37, 38, 41, 42, 59, 74

FOREWORD

BY JOHN S. EVANS QPM, LL.B

Chief Constable of the Devon & Cornwall Constabulary

In June 1997 the Devon and Cornwall Constabulary celebrated its 30th Anniversary. With the new century fast approaching this is an appropriate time to look back and reflect upon the achievements of former officers in the two counties, those who helped to shape the modern-day police force.

The threat of danger is an ever-present factor in policing and has existed since professional police officers first appeared in the West Country in the last century. These dangers can come in many forms and our predecessors faced challenges, unknown to us today, without the aid of the technology we now take for granted. Acts of bravery in which officers have risked their lives doing their duty can easily be forgotten as time passes; the nature of the work is such that we rarely allow ourselves time to remember.

This book is a tribute to all our former colleagues who performed acts of gallantry in the course of their careers, or in the service of their country in time of war. Their deeds must not be forgotten and I hope this record will serve to remind police officers currently serving in the Devon and Cornwall of the proud tradition they have inherited; and to show the community we seek to serve that their trust in us has not been misplaced.

John Evans
Chief Constable

ACKNOWLEDGEMENTS

I have been fortunate enough to spend time with some of the officers included in this book and speak to others or their relatives where they are no longer with us. I would like to extend my thanks to them all, and also to others who have helped in some way. I have found people nothing but very willing to put themselves out to answer some, often very minor, questions or to research obscure facts from many years ago.

My thanks go to Arthur Brown BEM, John Evans DSO, Frank Naughton GC, Richard Pitts DFC, Arthur McCartney DFC QPM, Mrs Peggy Jenkins, widow of John Jenkins DFC for her stories of the life of a policeman's wife in the post-war years, Peter Dunsford for relating his experiences as a prisoner of war in Germany and Poland, and lastly Lt Col. (Retd) Bob Roberts BEM and Mr Murphy, both of the Devonshire Regimental Museum, Exeter - all gave up their time when I visited them.

There were others to whom I spoke or wrote who also have my gratitude. They include: The Chevalier Ted Burnell; Retired Assistant Chief Constable Ken Back; Miss Rita Mayer, archivist at the RSPCA Head Office in Sussex; retired Chief Superintendent R J Perryman for the information about his father; David Fletcher of the Tank Museum, Bovington, Dorset; former Chief Superintendent E A Dickaty of the Plymouth City Police whose history of that force was invaluable in pointing me in the right direction once or twice; Mrs Mary Tucker, widow of Bill Tucker DFM; John Edwards of the RAF Museum, Hendon; Miss Perkin, niece of Harry Turner KPM; and former Chief Superintendent Jack Shepherd for the phone calls and copy documents. The more obscure questions posed to the Carnegie Hero Fund Trust, Dunfermline and the Commonwealth War Graves Commission were answered swiftly and I am grateful for the help of Navy News, Westcountry TV, local radio stations and newspapers although, unfortunately, the mystery of the DSC was never solved.

There were many others in regimental archives and museums who also helped and supplied copies of their crests or cap badges used in the chapters relating to honours won in the two world wars.

I must make special mention of Brian Estill, curator of the Force museum - he never complained when I pestered him for access to his records, asked him a trivial question, or wandered in and out of his office with box after box of his treasured files, papers and photographs to take way and peruse at my leisure.

Finally I must acknowledge the indulgence granted to me by the Chief Constable, John S Evans QPM, LLB, Chief Superintendent David Webb, and Superintendent Pat Grimley, and the patience and encouragement of my wife, Joy, who never complained as I talked incessantly about the whole project and each new tale I uncovered.

INTRODUCTION

The present Devon and Cornwall Constabulary has responsibility for the greater part of the south-west peninsula including the Isles of Scilly. The Force was formed in June 1967 on the amalgamation of the three police forces which then existed in the region - the Devon and Exeter Constabulary, Plymouth City Police and the Cornwall Constabulary, each of these having grown from earlier consolidations of smaller forces since the time that professional police officers were first seen in the West Country in the mid nineteenth century. As the idea of organised policing grew and became accepted a number of borough forces were formed, usually with very few officers and limited areas of responsibility.

The City of Plymouth, as an example, was once policed by three separate forces: Plymouth Borough Police, Devonport Borough Police and the Stonehouse Division of the Devon County Constabulary, until they were amalgamated into the Plymouth City Constabulary in November 1914. The Force grew over the years as the city expanded into areas of Devon still policed by the county force - areas such as Plympton and Plymstock which were only recently absorbed by the city. The area now under the control of the Plymouth City Council forms a single division of the Devon and Cornwall Constabulary.

Early amalgamations of smaller forces in Devon had subsumed several very small forces - the South Molton Borough Police with its two officers joined the Devon County Constabulary in October 1877 taking a lead from Torrington in 1870 also with two officers and followed by officers from forces at Totnes (three), Tiverton (seven), Bideford (two), Barnstaple (ten) and others.

In Cornwall a number of small, separate forces that included Truro, Penryn, Falmouth, Helston and Penzance also existed and were similarly consolidated into an ever growing county force until the mid twentieth century when a single force was established to police all Cornwall. These amalgamations culminated in the final act of 1967 from which was formed the present Constabulary.

The job of a police officer has undergone even greater changes - there is no comparison between the duties expected of today's constables and those undertaken by their predecessors. The workload has increased beyond measure, the range and complexity of the law they are expected to know and enforce has grown steadily and the breadth of skills needed to police the ever-changing and more demanding society of the last years of the millennium is impossible to list fully.

One thing has, however, remained constant - the need for officers to act decisively in situations of extreme danger requiring courage and strength of character beyond that normally expected - and their willingness to do so. Many occupations are dangerous, few would deny that those who make a living at sea, miners and a host of others face the possibility of danger daily in the normal course of their working lives. Victims of crime, especially crimes of violence or other personal assaults, display levels of courage which often surprise themselves; police officers, however, accept the possibility of being required to act above and beyond the call of duty and, very occasionally, risk their lives, as a fundamental part of their job. Most officers would happily serve their full thirty years to retirement without ever having to do so but, thankfully not often, some of them have no choice and are rarely, if ever, found wanting.

Many acts of courage go unnoticed, unreported or unrecognised; officers are modest, they understand that their work can be dangerous and, when called upon to act, they accept the responsibility and the risk. This book is intended to record those acts of gallantry performed by police officers who have served in the police forces of Devon and Cornwall which have been formally recognised by the award of a national decoration, medal or honour - it does not include the many occasions when the Chief Constable has rewarded officers with his personal commendation in circumstances where the deed has not perhaps warranted a recommendation to the Home Secretary that a national award is appropriate or where such an honour has been refused.

Police officers are civilians, eligible for awards for bravery in similar fashion to any other member of the community. Deciding the most appropriate award in any given set of circumstances takes into consideration a number of factors including but not wholly dependent upon the level of danger involved and the risk of death faced by the recipient.

The highest honour is the **George Cross** followed by the **George Medal, Queen's Gallantry Medal** and, finally, the **Queen's Commendation for Brave Conduct**. None of these awards is exclusive to police officers; they can be won by anyone, including members of the Armed Forces where the act occurs in peacetime or there is not a more appropriate military award.

There was one other award available for police officers alone, the **Queen's Police Medal for Gallantry**, now only awarded posthumously and thankfully rare. This award was in effect the equivalent of the George Medal for police officers who lost their lives. The latter could not be awarded posthumously until November 1977 when an amendment to the Royal Warrant changed this, effectively rendering the Queen's Police Medal for Gallantry redundant. It has not since been awarded.

Over the years other awards have been made most frequently the **British Empire Medal for Gallantry**, won by several officers in Devon and Cornwall but now discontinued.

The risk of death is an important factor - the award of the George Cross would require such a risk of 90 to 100 per cent, the George Medal 50 to 90 per cent, the Queen's Gallantry Medal up to 50 per cent and the Commendation up to 20 per cent to merit consideration.

During the two world wars many police officers left their careers to serve in the Armed Forces. Most returned safely to their forces, many sporting medal ribbons as testimony to acts of bravery or devotion to duty performed in the service of their country. Details are included in the two chapters devoted to the wars as a tribute to all officers who took the King's shilling but, in particular, those who never returned. Any record of policing in the two counties and the officers who have served would be incomplete without some reference to them.

I have not included details of all officers who died on active service or as a result of enemy action during the Second World War; those who are mentioned are there for a specific purpose, as an example of the dangers faced in those special times. Similarly, other officers have died on duty, sometimes as a result of criminal activity - they too are excluded unless they were honoured with a national award.

Records held by the present Force are far from complete and information relating to former officers can be scarce even in those cases where the award was relatively recent and made for an act performed during an officer's police service. In some cases a wealth of information relating to the officer, his career and the circumstances in which he won the award is available. In others, very little can be gleaned apart from a few personal details and the fact that the honour was won. Inevitably there are gaps in the information available and there will be omissions, officers who should be included will have been overlooked - unfortunately this was unavoidable.

This is particularly true of the Special Constabulary, Police War Reserve and First Police Reserve. **Police War Reserve Miners**, of the **Cornwall Constabulary**, for example, was awarded the **King's Commendation for Brave Conduct** on 5 November 1941 for removing the pilot from a burning aircraft - there is no information held about the officer, his career or his actions in the Force. There are undoubtedly others who have been overlooked.

THE GEORGE CROSS

The George Cross stands in a class of its own in the Order of Precedence for Honours - second only to the Victoria Cross. It is the highest honour for bravery that can be won by a civilian and is awarded only where the most conspicuous courage was displayed, where the recipient was in the most extreme danger - a likelihood of death of 90 to 100 per cent.

The Cross was instituted in September 1940 by King George VI, primarily to recognise acts of bravery performed during the Blitz on London and other towns and cities, and has only been awarded on approximately 180 occasions since, such is the level of bravery required. Servicemen and women are eligible for the Cross where the act occurs in peacetime or where there is not a more suitable purely military honour but it is generally regarded as a civil honour and often popularly referred to as the Civilian VC.

The Cross is cast in silver with a central medallion containing the figure of St George fighting the Dragon surrounded with the legend 'for Gallantry' - and hangs from a plain blue ribbon. Holders have the right to use the initials GC after their name.

Frank NAUGHTON
(Plymouth City)

As holder of the George Cross Frank Naughton has the distinction of being the most highly decorated officer to serve with the police force in Devon or Cornwall.

He joined the Plymouth City Police as Constable 257 on 10 March 1938 after serving as a private (No. 7882964) with the Royal Tank Corps from 21 July 1931 to October 1937. He was recalled to the Colours on 1 December 1939, serving throughout the Second World War, mainly in India and Burma, until he was discharged with the rank of captain from the 150th Yorks and Lancs Royal Armoured Corps.

He returned to Plymouth after the war and stayed with the Force until his retirement on 9 March 1968 from the Devon and Cornwall Constabulary. His whole service was spent in the city, serving at the Octagon until his call-up and at Greenbank after his return from the Army. The first nine years of his second spell of service were spent on the beat at Greenbank followed by eight years in the Charge Office and six in the Process Office until his retirement. Frank Naughton won his award during his first period of military service in India:

On 5 August 1936 two men of the 10th Light Tank Co were engaged in recovering an armoured car which had broken down on the Irish Bridge over the flooded River Indrayani, near Moshi (India) when they were swept off the bridge into the water below, where there were very swift and dangerous currents. Private Naughton, who was fully clothed except for his boots, immediately dived off the bridge to render assistance. Exhausted by the strong cross and underwater currents and unable to find either man, he had managed to regain shallow water. When he saw one of the soldiers appear on the surface about 40 yards away, he again entered the river and by extraordinary efforts succeeded in bringing the man ashore 100 yds downstream.

For his actions Frank Naughton was awarded the **Empire Gallantry Medal** (EGM) on 1 February 1937.

The Medal was presented to him in a grand ceremony at Poona Racecourse, India by the Governor of Bombay.

When the George Cross was instituted one condition of the Royal Warrant was that living holders of the EGM should be invited to exchange their medal for the GC - Frank Naughton was one of those affected. His investiture and the presentation of his George Cross by the King took place at Buckingham Palace in February 1947.

Today the Royal Tank Corps honours former members who won the VC or GC by naming light tanks of the Reconnaissance Regiment after them - there are six VCs and two GCs - including Frank Naughton - remembered by the Corps on the Scimitar light tank *Naughton GC*.

THE GEORGE MEDAL

The George Medal was instituted at the same time as the George Cross and is awarded in circumstances which are similar but are not so outstanding as to merit the award of the higher honour, a decision usually but not exclusively dependent upon the degree of danger involved and the risk of death. Consequently, the medal is awarded more freely than the George Cross but still demands a high degree of courage. It is worn before the Queen's Police Medal for Gallantry and after the Conspicuous Gallantry Medal - an RAF award.

The Medal is cast in silver with the name of the holder inscribed on the rim and hangs from a red ribbon with five narrow dark blue stripes. Holders are entitled to the use of the initials GM after their name.

Derek Raymond Alan HARPER
(Devon)

In a few hours on the night of Friday 15 August 1952 the peaceful town of Lynmouth on the North Devon coast became the scene of utter devastation with a loss of life unparalleled in peacetime in Devon or Cornwall.

Situated where the East and West Lyn rivers meet and enter the Bristol Channel, this town of barely 1800 inhabitants was hit by a torrent of water with unimaginable force. In a short space of time almost nine inches of rain fell on Exmoor and, inevitably, led to flooding of the two rivers in the valley above Lynmouth. By the time the flood reached the town, trees had been uprooted, boulders dislodged and all manner of debris swept along towards the sea.

Bridges were destroyed, roads washed away and houses severely damaged, all coming to a head in the town as the water crashed down from the hills behind. When daylight came and the waters subsided 39 houses and hotels had vanished completely or been totally destroyed and a further 149 damaged beyond repair; nine road bridges were destroyed, 14 others badly damaged and 19 roads made impassable. In addition, 94 cars, lorries and caravans were washed out to sea, 74 others submerged and 19 boats simply disappeared from the harbour.

Loss of life was high - 34 people were swept away to their deaths, including two holidaymakers from Australia, a child of three and a baby. Four bodies were never recovered and one lady remained unidentified.

This was the scene which greeted the three constables from the nearest police station at Lynton at the top of the hill. All communication had failed, any help would be some time arriving and their task was all but impossible. They worked continuously throughout the flood, leading and co-ordinating the rescue effort until help arrived, many hours later.

Individual acts of courage tended to be lost or overlooked amongst the almost overwhelming chaos and the immediate needs of those affected, but some were recorded. At the height of the storm Derek Harper and six of the retained firemen on duty responded to a report that a lady was trapped in the cellar of a house and in danger of drowning. With a great deal of difficulty caused by the flooded roads and damaged bridges they succeeded in reaching the cottage and there heard the lady's cries for help from the cellar. She was up

Above: *Barbrook Cottages, Lynmouth, where four cottages were washed away.*

Right: *Devastation at Lynmouth following the floods of August 1952.*

Left and below: *scenes in the stricken village in the aftermath of the Lynmouth flood disaster, 1952.*

to her neck in water and prevented from escaping by a mass of debris floating in the water.

Constable Harper and two of the firemen went into the cellar, waded chest deep in water until they reached her and managed to take her to safety. Shortly afterwards Derek Harper attempted to cross the badly damaged Barbrook Bridge at the end of a rope tied to his waist but was prevented from doing so by the force of the water - the bridge began to break up as he was crossing, placing him in great danger until he was hauled back to safety. He made his way to Lynmouth and took charge of the situation on the east side of the West Lyn River until help could arrive many hours later.

A second group of rescuers - people from all walks of life including Constables Pavey and Earle - was concerned in three separate operations. Some 45 to 50 people were evacuated from the Lyn Valley Hotel which was cut off and in great danger of collapsing.

Some time later several people, including a lady of 84 years, were found trapped on the upper floor of a cottage, also crumbling and in danger of being swept away. Using ropes and a ladder, four members of the party succeeded in

Constables Earl and Harper.

getting across to the cottage to take the trapped people to safety - eight others were rescued from an adjoining cottage shortly afterwards by Constable Earle and three of the party.

Statements taken after the disaster were confused and disjointed making it almost impossible to say clearly which member of the rescue group was responsible for which individual act of courage - each took risks and placed his own life in danger at a time when the storm was raging, it was totally dark with the noise and confusion making communication next to impossible.

Constable Pavey was working under the additional stress of knowing that his wife, Beryl, was involved somewhere in the flood with no idea whether or not she was safe.

The work of the three officers was recognised on 30 December 1952 with notification of their awards (*London Gazette* 26 December 1952):

for courage, leadership and devotion to duty in extremely hazardous conditions on the occasion of the floods in Devonshire and Somerset during August, 1952.

Constable 399 Derek Harper was awarded the George Medal for his part in the rescue operation. He was 24 years old and a probationer (joined 27 June 1951) with a bare 14 months service in August 1952. He joined the Police Service after his National Service with the Royal Artillery (October 1946 to 1948) and three months with the Kenya Police between February and May 1951. After leaving Lynton he served at Crediton, Exeter and Cullompton amongst others until he was promoted to sergeant. He served for some time in the Training Department in South Devon and, later, in North Devon until his retirement on 11 April 1977. He remained with the Force as a member of the Support Staff until he finally left in May 1993.

Constable 177 James Hudson Earle (39 years) and Constable 246 Stanley Harold James PAVEY (31 years), the two other officers involved, were both awarded the British Empire Medal for Gallantry for the rôle they played.

James Earle joined the Constabulary on 1 October 1933 and spent the early years of his service at Brixham, Tavistock and Ide. On 22 July 1946 he was seconded to the Control Commission in Germany for 12 months being posted to

James Earl.

Ashburton for two months on his return before moving to Lynton on 9 September 1947. He was promoted to sergeant on 1 November 1952 and to inspector exactly six years later. He retired on 3 October 1963.

Stanley Pavey joined the Constabulary on 3 May 1946 at the end of six years war service with the Royal Army Medical Corps and was posted to Lynton in March 1949 after time spent at Bideford and Strete.

During his military service, after VE Day, he spent some time working in the concentration camp at Belsen and saw at first hand the results of the atrocities committed there.

He was twice honoured in his police career by the Royal Humane Society for saving life, both events occurring in 1952 - an eventful year. He received a testimonial on parchment on 24 March for saving the life of a woman from cliffs at Countisbury, North Devon - with James Earle, also similarly honoured - and, in November, he was awarded the RHS Bronze Medal and Certificate for the rescue of two people from cliffs at Lynton in August.

Stanley Pavey was promoted to sergeant on 7 November 1957 but sadly died in service at Totnes on 6 September 1969.

The part played by others was also recognised by the award of two further British Empire Medals and the Queen's Commendation for Brave Conduct to nine people involved including Constable James Claude Hutchings of the Somerset Constabulary, stationed at Exford.

Richard Joseph Smale WILLIS
(Plymouth City)

Richard Willis received the George Medal on 19 November 1943 for his actions during the Blitz on the city on 12 August 1943; the only such award to a serving officer of the Plymouth City Police. He was born on 17 December 1910 and joined the City Force on 16 June 1930. Apart from a spell spent with the RAF during the Second World War, he served until 31 September 1960, retiring as an inspector to take up employment as a court usher at Plymouth Magistrate's Court. He died, aged 74, on 13 January 1985.

During the Blitz in Plymouth and other UK towns and cities, firewatchers performed their potentially very dangerous task night after night, alone or in twos, in exposed positions at the mercy of the German bombers. On the night of 12 August 1943 two firewatchers became trapped in a building in Union Street which had suffered a direct hit.

Richard Willis was on duty close by and, almost as a matter of routine, ran to the building to take charge of any rescue operation that might be necessary. Often, none was needed but, on this occasion, his help was vital. The first firewatcher was quickly found and pulled from the debris but the other was trapped beneath tons of rubble, only his arm visible.

Assisted by an American Merchant Sailor, Marian Jaskowski, a former member of the Polish Navy, Constable Willis climbed to the first floor of the building where they both crossed the eight foot gap to the trapped man using a number of planks of wood salvaged from the wrecked building. They worked for over an hour in a confined space before eventually successfully freeing the trapped firewatcher and taking him to safety. Only moments after he had been freed the building collapsed totally, throwing tons of masonry on to the very spot where they had been working. Sadly, the firewatcher later died of his injuries.

Richard Willis was awarded the George Medal by King George VI at an investiture at Buckingham Palace on 14 March 1944. Some six years after his death, on 27 June 1991, his son, Brian, then a resident of the United States, presented his father's medals to the Chief Constable at Force Headquarters, Middlemoor.

Left and above: *scenes from the Plymouth Blitz.*

For his part in the rescue the US sailor was awarded an honorary **British Empire Medal for Gallantry**. British orders, decorations and medals are intended primarily for award to British Subjects and members of the Commonwealth (formerly the Empire). This extends to the different classes of membership of the Order of the British Empire - including the Medal - and, as a United States citizen, Marian was not eligible for formal membership. His brave actions, however, and the help given to Richard Willis, merited some form of recognition and the BEM was considered to be the most appropriate in the circumstances. To overcome the constitutional difficulties, the award of the medal was given 'honorary' status.

Victor William HUTCHINGS
(Exeter City)

When the Second World War broke out in 1939 many police forces increased their strength by calling up war reserve constables to meet the increased demands and duties the war would undoubtedly bring to bear on the regular officers. In Devon, two days after war was declared, the Chief Constable, Major L H Morris MC, called up 100 such officers. Similar arrangements, although to a lesser extent, were made in the other forces of the region.

Many war reserve constables were former regular officers, usually retired constables and sergeants, whose skills, expertise and experience could be used in support of regular officers. As the war progressed others were recruited direct from civilian life to bolster the regular strength or replace officers who had left to join the Armed Forces. There was no difference between the duties expected of regular officers or war reserve officers and no difference between the dangers they faced.

William John Cheek served with the Plymouth City Police for 25 years from 8 October 1907 to 12 October 1932 as Constable 148. There was something of a

Bomb damage in Fore Street, Exeter; looking towards Exe Bridge.

More scenes of devastation following air raids on Exeter. The major raids began in May 1942 and continued sporadically until the middle of the following year.

policing tradition in the family - a brother served with the Metropolitan Police and his son with the Devon Constabulary from 1937 to 1967. On 16 May 1938 with war threatening in Europe he joined the Plymouth City First Police Reserve as Constable 405. He was killed on duty as a result of enemy action during an air attack on Plymouth on 21 April 1941.

Victor William Hutchings was a war reserve constable with the Exeter City Police who won the George Medal for his actions in 1942 following a bombing raid over the city. Together with Ernest William Howard, a civil defence warden, he rescued five people trapped in a cellar in Verney Place, Exeter:

> *When a high explosive bomb demolished a house, fires broke out and five persons were trapped in a cellar under a mass of bricks and debris. A narrow chute which led into the cellar from the road was blocked with bricks and smouldering wreck-age. Howard and Hutchings who had both, earlier in the night, displayed consid-erable courage and initiative in dealing with fires and in rescuing people from wrecked and burning houses, attempted to reach the cellar from inside the house, but smoke and flames drove them out. They then removed hot bricks and rubble from the entrance to the chute and first Howard, then Hutchings entered the cellar which was full of smoke and fumes. Howard brought out a newly-born baby, and then went back and rescued a crippled man by carrying him up the chute on his back. He then led out another man. Hutchings, although almost overcome by smoke, meanwhile was able to release and carry out a man and a woman. Warden Howard and Constable Hutchings displayed outstanding bravery in effecting the rescues which were carried out in the face of enormous difficulties and danger. After their efforts both men carried on throughout the rest of the night, Howard acting as a messenger for the Fire Service and Hutchings performing police duties.*

(*London Gazette*, 25 Sept 1942)

THE ORDER OF THE BRITISH EMPIRE

The structure of the Most Excellent Order of the British Empire is complex with a number of classes of membership including Members (MBE), Officers (OBE) and Commanders (CBE). Admission to the Order was mostly reserved for senior officers under the class structure applicable to the award of orders, decorations and medals during the war years and until very recently.

The second major conflict of the twentieth century had, in many ways, a more direct effect on the civilian population of the country than the mindless slaughter of the Great War. The impact of the bombing campaign conducted against the towns and cities of the south-west brought home to everyone the realities of modern warfare. The cities of Exeter and Plymouth suffered as greatly as any other from the death and destruction caused by air raids. The raids placed a new burden on the Police Service and those officers not recalled to the Armed Forces faced challenges and dangers previously unknown. Countless acts of bravery took place and many were recognised by the award of decorations, orders, medals and commendations.

Three officers from Plymouth were appointed as 'Additional Members of the Civil Division of the Most Excellent Order of the British Empire' in recognition of the part they played during the Blitz on the city in 1941.

On 25 July 1941, Cecil Charles Cooper, Divisional Commandant of Plymouth City Special Constabulary, was appointed with a citation published in the *London Gazette* of that date:

> *During air raids Mr. Cooper has given valuable assistance to the regular services. On one occasion he searched houses for trapped persons and salvaged stocks of food from premises wrecked and on fire. Mr. Cooper showed courage and an undaunted public spirit during long periods of duty under exacting conditions, attendant always with the risk of grave personal injury, and, by his splendid example, he gave added encouragement to those working around him.*

In addition to Cecil Cooper, two regular officers were appointed as Members of the Order on 19 September 1941 (*London Gazette*, page 5397): they were Alexander Bertram Hawkins and John Philip William Hingston.

Alexander Hawkins was a native of Clapham, London (born 22 June 1895) who moved to Plymouth joining the City Force on 20 February 1919 after almost four years army service with the Royal Field Artillery.

His career saw him move steadily through the ranks to retire on pension on 25 February 1945 with the rank of superintendent.

In 1932, as a sergeant, he was commended by the Chief Constable, Watch Committee and City Council for his part in the quelling of the mutiny at Dartmoor Prison on 24 January.

At the time of the Blitz in 1941 he had reached the rank of superintendent in command of the Eastern Division and played a major role in the police response to this new challenge for the Police Service. The *London Gazette* entry notifying his appointment carried a citation:

During enemy air attacks on Plymouth Superintendent Hawkins constantly patrolled his division which suffered severe damage from bombs and fire. He led parties in rescue work, directed the salvage of goods and helped to fight fires. His excellent qualities of leadership and courage have had a stimulating influence on the men working under him, and he has carried out his duty regardless of his own safety.

John Hingston was a local man who rose through the ranks of the Police Service in his native Plymouth to be appointed Deputy Chief Constable with the substantive rank of chief superintendent on 19 December 1941.

He applied for the post of Chief Constable in 1943 but was denied the opportunity of reaching the very top in his home force by a single vote in the Watch Committee - a major disappointment to him.

He joined the Force on 6 November 1919 after four years with the Army during the Great War and served in the Police War Department and as the Force Hackney Carriage Inspector in addition to normal uniformed duties. He formed the first Traffic Department in Plymouth in 1937 as an inspector.

At the time of the Blitz he was the superintendent in command of the Western Division.

The citation published in the *London Gazette* appointing him to Membership of the Order gave brief details of his duties during the bombing campaign conducted against the city:

Throughout the air raids on Plymouth, Superintendent Hingston, by splendid co-ordination of effort, resourcefulness and organising ability, has maintained effective control of the most important and serious incidents in his division. He has displayed courage and cheerfulness in circumstances involving considerable personal risk, sharing to the full the dangers and discomforts of the men under his command.

In the early years of his service he was commended once by the Chief Constable for his services during the coal strike in Glamorgan and once by the Justices of Plymouth Police Court for help given to two people rescued from drowning at Whitsand Bay.

On 10 June 1948, seventeen months before his retirement from the Force, he was awarded the King's Police and Fire Service Medal for Distinguished Service. John Hingston retired in November 1949 and died on 12 February 1976.

THE BRITISH EMPIRE MEDAL FOR GALLANTRY

The history of the British Empire Medal is quite involved - the name and criteria for its award having undergone a number of changes since its inception in 1917.

The first version was changed in 1922 with the introduction of two separate medals:

(a) The Medal of the Order of the British Empire for Gallantry, more commonly known as the Empire Gallantry Medal (EGM).

(b) The Medal of the Order of the British Empire for Meritorious Service.

With the introduction of the George Cross in 1940, the Empire Gallantry Medal was abolished and living holders were ordered to return their award and receive the new medal in its place.

The criteria for the award of the British Empire Medal for meritorious service were changed to include acts of gallantry but the design of the medal and its title were the same. In December 1957 an emblem of crossed silver oakleaves was introduced to be worn on the ribbon to signify that it was awarded for gallantry.

In 1974 the Queen's Gallantry Medal was introduced to recognise the differences that existed between the criteria necessary for the award of the BEM and to acknowledge the special circumstances of acts of bravery as distinct from those awarded for more general acts of service. The award of the BEM for gallantry ceased.

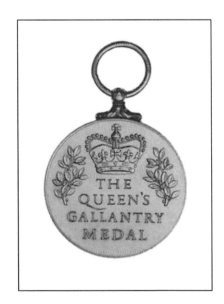

A number of officers who served in Devon and Cornwall, the constituent forces or other forces prior to transferring to the south-west have been awarded the BEM for Gallantry.

John Frederick William LINDSEY
(Plymouth City)

John Lindsey joined the Plymouth City Constabulary on 6 November 1919 after serving with the Army for seven years. He retired with the rank of inspector 30 years later on 13 November 1949.

In the early years of his service, as Constable 29, he was commended three times by his Chief Constable. The first came on 1 January 1926 when he was 'commended by the Chief Constable for prompt action and attention to duty in discovering a fire at 18 Drake Street late on the night of the 31st December 1925'.

Fifteen months later, on 22 March 1927, he was again commended by the Chief Constable for 'services in connection with the coal strike in Glamorganshire'.

The third recognition of his work was noted in his personal file on 1 February 1928 when he was 'commended by the Chief Constable on the 16th January 1928, for affecting the arrest of two soldiers for larceny and wilful damage'.

Constable Lindsey was promoted to sergeant on 20 October 1932 and on 18 November 1936, shortly after achieving 16 years service, he was awarded the Plymouth City Constabulary's Good Service Medal by the Watch Committee.

Prior to 1951 when the present national Police Long Service and Good Conduct Medal was instituted, many forces made their own awards to officers - mostly of different designs and with different ribbons.

As the medals were not nationally recognised they were worn on the right side of the tunic. These awards were discontinued in 1951 as a condition of the Royal Charter introducing the current medal, although many forces had long since ceased issuing them. Both the Plymouth City and Exeter City Forces issued their own medals.

Both Devon's major cities suffered heavy damage during the Second World War. These pictures show the effects of bombing on private housing and industrial premises.

The Plymouth City medal, minted in silver, showed the arms of the city of the obverse with the name of the Force and the legend 'Good Service' on the reverse. There was also space for the name of the recipient to be engraved but this was a matter for officers to have done at their own expense and, consequently, many are blank. The ribbon is red with two broad dark blue stripes towards the edges and a narrow dark blue stripe in the centre. The medal was introduced in Plymouth in 1930 by Archibald Kennedy Wilson, the Chief Constable from 1929 to 1932, and remained in use until 1951.

Later in his service, during the Second World War, on 15 October 1941, John Lindsey was awarded a bar to his medal 'for services during an air raid on Plymouth in March 1941'. The bar was inscribed with the legend 'for Gallantry'.

The award of the bar was prompted by an earlier, more prestigious honour bestowed on Inspector John Lindsey. On 25 July 1941 he had been awarded the British Empire Medal for Gallantry for his actions following an air attack on the City Hospital at Greenbank:

> *During an air raid the City Hospital, Plymouth, was struck by high explosive bombs. Children and nurses were trapped beneath the debris which caught fire, causing dense smoke and fumes. Bombs continued to fall nearby but despite these dangers and difficulties Inspector Lindsey directed rescue operations and, under his able and courageous leadership, the police rescued nine children.*

He was presented with the medal by King George VI at an investiture at Buckingham Palace on 2 December 1941. Both John Lindsey's medals are on display at the current Divisional Headquarters at Crownhill, Plymouth.

William Cecil MARSHALL
Terrence Albert O'CONNOR,
Frederick Samuel STANLEY
Alfred Henry DEARING
(Plymouth City)

The three regular officers and one member of the Special Constabulary (Alfred Dearing) were each awarded the BEM for Gallantry for their courage during an intensive air raid on Plymouth in 1941. This was the greatest number of honours ever awarded to police officers in the city arising from a single event (four officers from the Cornwall Constabulary, however, had each won the King's Police Medal for Gallantry before the War). The *London Gazette*, 25 July 1941, page 4255, carried a citation:

> *During a severe air attack these Constables were on duty in the City. Business premises were hit by high explosive and incendiary bombs and many fires broke out. While the raid was still intensive, the men were actively engaged in rescue work, liberating many people and rendering first aid to the injured. The four Constables, who were in considerable danger the whole time from high explosive bombs and from the collapse of buildings, showed commendable courage and devotion to duty.*

Constable 263 Stanley initially joined the Metropolitan Police on 15 July 1935, transferring to Plymouth City on 19 May 1938, three days after he voluntarily resigned from London. He was commended three times by the Chief Constable during his service in Plymouth for his perseverance and ability investigating offences of warehousebreaking, receiving stolen goods and managing a brothel, all resulting in convictions at Plymouth City Police Court. Frederick Stanley served in Plymouth for eight years, resigning at his own request on 5 May 1946.

William Marshall was born in Roche, Cornwall on 1 June 1907 and joined the Force on 6 July 1933 (Constable 150). He never sought promotion and retired on pension after 25 years service on 13 July 1958. During his service he was commended twice by his Chief Constable for ability, efficiency and enthusiasm and once by the Coroner on 2 September 1947 for:

the painstaking enquiries he had made, and on the clear and concise manner in which he gave evidence in connection with the inquest of J Burston - fatal accident 23.6.47.

Terrence O'Connor, a native of Stratford, London, joined the Plymouth City Police (PC 239) at the age of 23 on 9 January 1936 staying for exactly 30 years until his retirement on pension with the rank of inspector on 8 January 1966.

He served in several branches of the Force including the Training Department and the CID in addition to uniformed duties at all three ranks attained. He was commended three times by his Chief Constable, on the first occasion for ability and enthusiasm investigating a series of road traffic offences committed by a group of six young men (5 February 1948) and later for his work which secured the conviction of three men for shopbreaking and receiving stolen goods.

On 4 May 1965, as an inspector, less than 12 months away from his retirement, he was commended for:

courage, tenacity and resourcefulness in affecting the arrest of a youth armed with a knife who had shown his willingness to use it to prevent his apprehension.

Terrence O'Connor was also once commended by the Chairman of the Bench at the local Magistrates' Court for:

ability and restraint shown by him in what he described as a 'difficult position' concerning four Royal Marines arrested for robbery.

The four men were later acquitted at the Assize Court.

After the end of the War, on Sunday 10 June 1945, Constable O'Connor BEM represented the Plymouth City Police at the Civil Defence and Allied Services Parade held in London.

Victor Charles COBLEY
(Plymouth City)

Constable 273 Cobley joined the Plymouth City Police on 3 April 1939 and rose to the rank of chief inspector at the time of his retirement from the Devon and Cornwall Constabulary on 30 September 1969.

During the Second World War he won the BEM for Gallantry (25 July 1941) for his actions during an air attack on the city in the Blitz. The *London Gazette* entry for that date carries a citation:

When a building at Plymouth was partly demolished by high explosive bombs, Constable Cobley worked hard and intelligently to rescue the casualties. He then helped to release several persons trapped in the basement of a private house. Completing this task, and whilst bombing was still active, he attended to the wants of victims bombed out of their homes. Further bombs dropped during this period and the Constable, with assistance, extricated three persons from a house that had received a direct hit and was on fire. This rescue was particularly hazardous and necessitated working with the greatest possible speed. Cobley continued his work, exhibiting a conspicuously high standard of conduct generally during the period of the raid.

Herbert William Davey BESWICK
Alan John Tucker HILL
(Plymouth City)

During 1941 when the Blitz on Plymouth was at its peak the primary duty of a police officer was the saving of life and most awards made for actions in this period were in recognition of that. It can sometimes, however, be overlooked that food was in short supply and the destruction of stocks by enemy action could have had a severe effect on life in the city.

Inspector Beswick and Constable 119 Hill were both awarded the British Empire Medal for Gallantry for saving a consignment of food after a railway wagon had been hit by incendiary bombs:

During an air raid incendiary bombs fell on a Goods Depot and ammunition trucks were set on fire. Nearby a wagon was burning in a shed, containing a large supply of food stuffs. It was essential that the wagon should be removed. Exploding ammunition was flying in all directions but, ignoring the danger to themselves, Inspector Beswick and Constable Hill entered the shed and managed to push the wagon to a position where it could do little damage. The courageous action of the two men saved a substantial quantity of food.

(London Gazette, 22 August 1941, page 4848)

The police careers of the two men were very different. Herbert Beswick joined the Force on 6 October 1927 and served for 31 years until his retirement on pension on 12 January 1958. He was promoted several times, rising steadily through the rank structure to reach the rank of superintendent in 1953.

Alan Hill, on the other hand, stayed in Plymouth for a very short time. He first joined the Metropolitan Police at the age of 19 on 17 June 1935 but resigned two years later to transfer to Plymouth on 12 May 1938.

During the war, on 16 February 1942, he enlisted in the RAF for training as a pilot and stayed for the duration. On 16 June 1946, without returning to Plymouth, he resigned from the Force to take up the offer of a permanent commission.

John Francis Cresswell PEACE
Arthur William LARSON
(Plymouth City)

John Peace, a native of Sidcup, Kent, born on 26 May 1916, joined the Plymouth City Police at the age of almost 22 after serving from 13 January 1936 to 8 May 1938 with the Metropolitan Police. In common with many other officers he was responding to an advert for constables placed by the Chief Constable of Plymouth in the years leading up to the outbreak of the Second World War. John Peace took up his post in Plymouth on 23 January 1936 and served with the Force until his retirement on pension on 31 May 1966.

His police career was interrupted during the war by a period spent with the Special Investigation Branch of the Corps of Military Police (No. 14248032) from

6 August 1942 until 16 December 1946 when he returned to Plymouth. He quickly rose through the ranks in the CMP, becoming an Acting Sergeant-Major on his transfer to the Army Reserve and return to the Police Service.

Arthur Larson was a member of the National Fire Brigade at the time of the Blitz in Plymouth. Before the war the local fire brigades, existing in most cities, were a part of the Police Force under the command of the Chief Constable. He originally joined the Police Force on 22 March 1928 and took up fire brigade duties on 6 April 1938.

He transferred to the National Brigade on 18 August 1941 as a Station Officer in the city, eventually being promoted to Company Officer, the rank he held on his return to the city police force on 1 November 1944 when the National Brigade was disbanded, as the war drew to a close, and the likelihood of air attack fell away.

Arthur Larson was a Fire Inspector with the Plymouth Police Fire Brigade when he and John Peace were awarded the British Empire Medal for Gallantry for their actions at the scene of a large fire caused by an enemy air attack:

> *Bombs caused several large fires at an Omnibus Depot. Fire Inspector Larson was in charge of the operations which were rendered difficult and dangerous by burning oil and exploding petrol tanks. Larson, Police Fireman Peace and Auxiliary Fireman Edgecombe took up the most dangerous positions and after three hours succeeded in subduing the flames. During the whole of this period high explosive and incendiary bombs were being dropped and the three men suffered considerably from the effect of blast and flying debris but refused to give up. They set a very fine example of fire fighting in conditions where there was great risk of death or injury.*

(*London Gazette*, 22 August 1941, page 4849)

Arthur Larson was commended once by the Chief Constable, on 14 November 1946, for ability and efficiency in making enquiries leading to the arrest and conviction of two men for a serious assault. He retired from the Police Service on pension on 25 March 1958.

John Peace received one commendation for his work in furtherance of road safety in particular involving children. In a period of 12 months he made more than 100 visits to schools and spoke to more than 30 000 children on the dangers they faced on the roads. His efforts were brought to the attention of the Chief Constable by parents, teachers and the Road Safety Committee resulting in the publication of the commendation on 11 December 1963.

William Thomas HILL
(Plymouth City)

William Hill was born in Saltash on 19 June 1899. He joined the Plymouth City Police in October 1920 after two years army service. On 1 April 1939 he was appointed as a fireman with the Police Fire Brigade under the joint arrangements then existing. Promoted to fire inspector in February 1941, he transferred to the National Fire Brigade after its formation in August the same year.

Two weeks before the transfer, on 1 August, he was awarded the British Empire Medal for Gallantry for his work in the city during the Blitz (*London Gazette* 1 August 1941, page 4416):

> *Awarded the British Empire Medal (Civil Division)*
> *William Thomas Hill, Inspector, Plymouth Police Fire Brigade.*
> *During an air raid a number of fires broke out. Inspector Hill at once began fire-fighting operations and was later joined by Chief Officer Drake of Stourport Fire*

Brigade in charge of several appliances and crews. Although at one time a large area was threatened by fire, these two Officers, by their masterly handling of the situation, prevented the fires from spreading and their courageous and persistent efforts resulted in much valuable property being saved. Chief Officer Drake and Inspector Hill showed courage and steadiness in very dangerous conditions and set a splendid example to their men.

During his police career, William Hill was twice commended by his Chief Constable for 'stopping a runaway horse in George Street on 18 July' (25 August 1923) and 'attention to duty in arresting two sailors for larceny and wilful damage' (1 February 1928).

On 1 April 1948, he resigned from the Force and joined the Plymouth Fire Brigade.

Clifford STROUD
(Plymouth City)

Clifford Stroud was an ambitious man, determined to rise to the top of his chosen profession. He joined the Plymouth City Police on 9 April 1923 and was first promoted less than 10 years later on 20 October 1932 as clerk sergeant. Further promotions followed and he attained the rank of superintendent on his retirement on 15 May 1956.

He applied for a number of vacancies advertised for superintendents and chief constables in forces as far afield as Southend-on-Sea, Hove, Cambridgeshire, Southampton and Penzance. He stayed in Plymouth, however, until his retirement.

In the course of his service he received a number of commendations including one from the Chief Constable, Watch Committee, City Council and the Home Secretary following the mutiny which took place at Dartmoor Prison on 24th January 1932.

On 25 July 1941 his personal record notes the award of the British Empire Medal for Gallantry for his conduct during air raids on the city in March and April the same year:

During intense air raids on the City of Plymouth, Inspector Stroud maintained effective control of operations in the bombed area. In extremely dangerous and difficult conditions he directed the rescue of many persons trapped in debris and in burning buildings. The inspector was several times blown off his feet and severely shaken by blast from H.E. bombs but, although suffering from exhaustion due to prolonged hours of duty, he continued to supervise and control police operations at many large incidents. By his display of courage and cool leadership he set a splendid example to the men under his command.

Robert Josiah Steer EAKERS
(Plymouth City)

Robert Eakers was a local man, born in the city on 5 May 1916, and joining his local force on 22 March 1928. He served for six months less than 30 years, retiring on pension on 8 August 1957 to take up a job at Freedom Fields Hospital. He died on 19 August 1970. Whilst still a probationer he was:

commended by the Justices at Plymouth Police Court on 8 October 1929 for his vigilance and attention to duty in a case of breaking and entering the premises of Messrs Spooners.

His career was unexceptional until the outbreak of war in 1939, and the commencement of the air attacks carried out on Plymouth, when he won the British Empire Medal for Gallantry for his conduct during one attack (*London Gazette* 3 September 1941):

> *During an air raid, high explosive bombs demolished houses. Constable Eakers entered one of the houses, the remaining walls and ceilings of which were likely to collapse, and found two casualties. He organised rescue parties and working with them removed five persons from the demolished property. Prior to this Constable Eakers had rescued a bedridden elderly woman from a house which was on fire. At considerable risk Eakers carried her down two flights of stairs to safety.*

On 15 October 1941 the Watch Committee recognised his actions with the award of the Plymouth City Police Conspicuous Bravery and Good Service Medal. On 6 October 1951 he was awarded the newly introduced national Long Service and Good Conduct Medal but, as a condition of the award, he was no longer entitled to wear the Plymouth City Medal.

Constable 227 Eakers received one further commendation during his career, on 22 October 1945, by the Chief Constable for: 'vigilance and keen attention to duty in the arrest of two escaped German prisoners of war'.

Daniel CRUTCHLEY
(Plymouth City)

Constable 45 Crutchley, a native of Stafford and a gardener by trade, joined the Plymouth City Police on 29 January 1931 and served for 31 years until his retirement on 18 March 1962 when he held the rank of inspector. In the course of his service he was commended four times by the Chief Constable for attention to duty and ability in connection with a numbers of arrests for offences of breaking and entering.

On 7 November 1941, Daniel Crutchley was awarded the British Empire Medal for Gallantry for his actions during an air raid in April the same year (*London Gazette*, page 6424):

> *A bomb demolished houses and persons were trapped in one of the basements. A large quantity of masonry and house timber, liable to collapse, was immediately over the spot at which it was necessary to begin rescue work. Regardless of this danger and the presence of coal gas, Constable Crutchley, working in a very limited space, started to remove the debris. He was partly overcome by the gas but after a brief rest continued until, five hours later, three men were rescued. Crutchley worked ceaselessly and untiringly for a further five hours in an attempt to rescue other casualties. It was due to the efforts, courage and initiative of the Constable that the three persons were rescued alive.*

PC Crutchley was assisted in his efforts by Special Constable Percy Thomas Gollop who was awarded the King's Commendation for Brave Conduct the same day. He was a local man who had been with the Special Constabulary since March 1939 and served in Plymouth throughout the Blitz.

Frederick John COX
(Plymouth Special Constabulary)

The role of the Special Constabulary during the war years cannot be underestimated and the actions of many members was recognised by the award of decorations, medals and commendations.

Frederick Cox, a special inspector in Plymouth, was awarded a Bar for Gallantry to his previously won British Empire Medal (Military Division) for his actions during an air raid in 1942:

Awarded a Bar (Civil Division) to the British Empire Medal:-

Frederick John Cox, B.E.M., Inspector, Plymouth Special Constabulary.

During a severe air raid Inspector Cox was off duty in a district which was heavily bombed. Many fires were started by incendiary bombs. and, appreciating the danger of the rapidly advancing flames in the congested area, the Inspector immediately organised fire parties. It was due to his efforts that the damage by fire was not more extensive. A store was demolished by a H.E. bomb and three persons were trapped. Inspector Cox led a rescue party which, after many hours of hard and dangerous work, during which bombs were dropped nearby, succeeded in extricating alive two of the trapped persons. Inspector Cox showed courage and devotion to duty.

(*London Gazette*, 24 April 1942, page 1806)

Prior to the Second World War there was no provision in the Royal Charter for the award of a Bar to the BEM. The change was made at the instigation of King George VI to ensure that the many acts of courage displayed during the Blitz were properly recognised.

George Harold SHAPTER
(Plymouth City)

Constable 40 Shapter served with the Plymouth City Police from 1 May 1919 until 31 December 1945, retiring on pension after 26 years. He was a local man, born in the city on 22 December 1898, and working as a lineman for the Post Office before joining the Force.

He encountered mixed fortunes in his early career being commended three times by the Justices and once by the Chief Constable but also finding himself subject to the harsh discipline of the times also on three occasions. He was very lucky once (16 February 1924) to escape dismissal from the Force for an offence of discreditable conduct in circumstances that would today, some 60 years later, barely cause an eyebrow to be raised within the Force, or the Community.

The circumstances of his three other brushes with the disciplinary code illustrate how times change; today two of the transgressions would not result in much more than a mild reprimand from an officer's sergeant, and the third would not be considered an offence at all.

On 11 February 1925, PC Shapter appeared before the Chief Constable on two charges of:

(1) Failing to report off duty at 10 pm, 10.2.25, and,

(2) Failing to report an occurrence either to his superior officer or in his official pocket book, 10.2.25.

He was found guilty on both charges and duly punished:

(1) Fined 10/- and loss of one days pay during suspension, and,

(2) Fined £1 and very severely reprimanded and cautioned (for the last time) and transferred to 'B' Division (Chief Constable's decision).

Some 11 years later he again appeared before the Chief Constable after failing to find a shop that had been broken into on his beat. He was fined £1 and had a service pay increment withdrawn for 'failing to work his beat in a proper manner'.

These were but lapses in the career of a otherwise keen, conscientious and able officer who showed his true self on 29 August 1944 when he performed an act of incredible bravery after an aircraft had crashed on to a train at Cattedown.

He was 44 years old at the time with his retirement imminent and the dangers caused by the air attacks of 1941 and 42 long past. The invasion of Normandy had taken place and the Allies were moving inexorably towards Germany with the end of the war almost in sight. George Shapter could be forgiven for thinking that the time might be right to take it easy for the last 12 months of his service.

At 4 pm on Tuesday, 29 August 1944, however, a 'Defiant' fighter-bomber (number 3434) of 691 Squadron of the RAF crashed on to a stationary goods train near Passage Wharf, Cattedown. It came to rest upside down on top of a truck containing drums of paraffin and caught fire after its fuel tanks exploded.

George Shapter was some 500 yards away at the time and, when he reached the scene, the aircraft was well alight with a very real danger that the paraffin would also catch fire or explode. The chances of either of the two crewmen being alive were slim.

George Shapter went straight up to the aircraft, looked inside, surrounded by the flames, and saw one crewman, still alive, about five feet away. He leaned into the aircraft and managed to pull the airman out and move him away from the flames. As he was about to re-enter the aircraft to help the pilot, it exploded, making any further help impossible. The airman pulled from the wreckage sadly died later in hospital and George Shapter was treated for burns and other injuries.

Witnesses testified to the total disregard he displayed for his own safety and he was subsequently recommended for the award of the George Cross by his Chief Constable. On 19 December 1944, he was awarded the British Empire Medal for Gallantry - notified in the Supplement to the *London Gazette*, 19 December 1944, page 5804.

Constable Shapter was assisted in the rescue attempt by two American seamen who were stationed at the US Naval Base at Martins Wharf: Emil Ludwig Weiss, aged 29 years, Seaman 2nd Class, USN (No. 8186913), and Daniel Buckley Yancey, aged 22 years, Motor Machinist 3rd Class, USN (No. 3686594),

They were subsequently both awarded the King's Commendation for Brave Conduct for the help given to George Shapter.

Daniel Yancey joined the US Navy at the age of 18 (born 15 May 1923) on 13 May 1941 and served in the European and Pacific theatres of the War. He came through unscathed and was discharged on 22 May 1946 in Los Angeles, California.

George Shapter was widowed in 1977 but re-married on 6 September 1979. Sadly he collapsed and died that same evening.

Kenneth John WALTERS
(Plymouth City)

Constable 262 Walters didn't win a gallantry award during the Blitz on Plymouth - he was killed by enemy action while on duty before the air raids reached full intensity. His story is included as an example of the dangers involved - if any is needed - and as a reminder that some officers paid the ultimate price.

Kenneth Walters was a native of Totnes (born 12 December 1916) who joined the Force at the age of 22 on 10 March 1938. He was one of a family of eight including an elder brother who was serving with the Devon Constabulary at Tavistock - Constable 152 Arthur Albert Walters.

At 9.30 pm on 21 April 1941 he paraded for night duty at Police Box 21 in Royal Navy Avenue in company with Constable 108 Reginald Hawkings, the late turn officer for the beat who was preparing to go off duty at 10 pm. When the air raid sirens sounded both officers checked their beat for any fires or damage which may have been caused by incendiary bombs. They made their way to the Corporation Gas Works in Keyham Road which was burning fiercely.

As they passed through Hamilton Street at about 10 o'clock a high explosive bomb fell on the opposite side of the street, a bare 25 yards away. The blast destroyed several houses and threw debris across the street partially burying the two officers.

PC Hawkings was stunned by the blast and lost consciousness, only remembering being treated later at the Prince of Wales Hospital in Devonport. He never saw Kenneth Walters alive again.

A resident of Keyham - George Edward Brett - who was on duty at his ARP post at the Gas Works witnessed the explosion and gave what little help he could to Kenneth Walters. His statement recorded by Sergeant 27 Miller on 3 May 1941 is short:

I am an A.R.P. Part-time at Post 6.A.1 (Gas Works, Keyham Rd). At about 10 pm Monday April 21st 1941 I was patrolling my sector during an air raid.
I was standing on the corner of the lane at the rear of Avondale Terr in Goschen St when I heard a H.E. bomb strike the houses in Hamilton St a distance of about 50 yards. Upon looking down the lane towards Hamilton St I saw a policeman staggering towards me. He was obviously in great pain and was supporting his stomach with his hands. He was hatless.
I immediately caught hold of him but neither of us spoke. I assisted him to the Public Air Raid Shelter at the rear of Goschen St, where he was treated by a young nurse whom I do not know. I went for an ambulance and after a while the policeman was taken to the Prince of Wales Hospital, Devonport.

Kenneth Walters was taken to the City Hospital for immediate surgery but never recovered from the severe abdominal wounds he had sustained - he died at 12.25 am on 23 April 1941.

Fourteen other officers died during the air raids on Plymouth in 1941 and 42 - four members of the regular force, five special constables, two members of the First Police Reserve and three from the Police War Reserve.

Ten weeks after Kenneth Walters lost his life, Constable 199 Walter James Brooks became the latest Plymouth City officer to die in the Blitz. The cause of his leaving the service is recorded simply in his personal record - 'Killed by enemy action at Devonport on 9th July 1941'.

He was a Devonport man, born in the Borough on 29 September 1908, who joined his local force, aged 23, on 31 December 1931, the day after his discharge from service with the Royal Engineers. After applications to the Devon County Constabulary and Metropolitan Police he chose Plymouth following in the footsteps of his father who had retired from a career as a constable in London eight years before. He spent all his police career at Devonport and developed into a 'clean and smart, very conscientious, loyal and obedient officer' who was twice commended by the Justices for 'vigilance and efficiency' in effecting the arrest of car thieves.

Walter Brooks was killed instantly by the blast from a high explosive bomb, with Police War Reserve Constable L Vicary, doing his duty in Devonport. He left a widow and four children including twins girls of 16 months.

In Exeter, a city which also suffered badly, one special constable, Harold Luxton, was killed by a bomb blast in Sidwell Street on 4 May 1942. In Devon

County, Area Officer Samuel Fisher Chetham and Special Constable Frederick George Pearse, were killed near Devon Square, Newton Abbot on 25 April 1942 by a high explosive bomb.

Arthur John BROWN
(Devon)

The Order of the British Empire (including the Medal) has two divisions - civil and military - with the former applying to awards made to serving police officers. The medals are of the same design and both hang from a salmon pink ribbon with a narrow grey stripe at each edge - the military division is identified by an additional narrow grey stripe running down the centre of the ribbon. During the war, the Medal was often given to soldiers, sailors and RAF personnel for acts of gallantry or meritorious service where a purely military award would have been the more usual form of recognition.

Arthur Brown was awarded the BEM (Military Division) on 28 June 1945 for gallantry and distinguished service in Italy. He started his police career with the Devon Constabulary (PC 120) on 1 April 1936 and served for 33 years, retiring on pension on 31 March 1969 from the Devon and Cornwall Force.

He had previously served with the Grenadier Guards from 20 March 1932 until 18 May 1935 and was recalled the Army on 1 December 1939 after war broke out. As a serving police officer he was transferred to the Corps of Military Police with many others in the same position and served as a Warrant Officer, Class II (acting) - No. 2613111. His police service started at Newton Abbot followed by a period at Sidmouth until he married and was sent to Slapton where he was stationed on his call-up in 1939.

Arthur Brown earned his BEM as a member of the Special Investigation Branch of the CMP for his part in a twelve month battle against organised crime in Rome after the city had been liberated in 1944.

When the Germans withdrew and the city was occupied by British and American troops, shortages of food, clothing and other commodities coupled with high prices and a flourishing black market led inevitably to high levels of crime.

Armed robbery for money and valuables carried out by gangs of criminals and deserters from all nations escalated out of the control of the civil police. Weapons were plentiful and the gangs were utterly ruthless - a deserter with very little to lose would shoot without hesitation if there was any resistance. Several deaths occurred before the Civil Authorities turned to the occupying forces for help.

A special squad, including Arthur Brown, from the British and American Military Police Corps was formed with orders to break the four gangs known to be responsible for the majority of serious crime.

Handicapped by the language difficulties in dealings with the local population and faced with the well-grounded fear of the gangs, gathering sufficient evidence to secure convictions was an immense task. Dogged detective work, the widespread use of informants, and a gradual trust built up between the authorities and the civilian population over many months, eventually yielded results - one gang was caught red-handed in a trap set at a gaming house acting on information received from an informant.

The life of informants was fraught with danger and the prospect of immediate death if discovered was very real. One was rescued by the squad at the very moment he was being bundled into a taxi by suspicious gang members for a journey from which he would never return.

After a year's work the gangs were broken and the ringleaders dealt with by military courts martial for a series of offences including robbery and murder. Five were executed, one of whom was a deserter (a petty officer) from the Royal Navy who became the last British serviceman to be shot by firing squad.

At the end of the war Arthur Brown was given the opportunity of staying with the Army with a commission but chose to return to the Police Service and was posted to Widecombe, to a police house with no electricity and no gas!

His police career was successful - he retired as a chief inspector. The two earlier promotions were both in the CID, from detective constable to detective sergeant on 1 November 1956 and to detective inspector on 1 February 1964.

During his CID career, which began with a move to Exmouth, he served at Torquay and Paignton as a detective sergeant, followed by promotion to detective inspector at Barnstaple, later returning to Torquay in charge of the Regional Crime Squad there. He ended his career as a chief inspector in command of the Southern Region (No 7), Regional Crime Squad.

Following his retirement from the Force he spent ten years as the part-time superintendent registrar at Newton Abbot. Arthur Brown died in Torquay on 27 March 1997.

John EMERSON
(Plymouth City)

John Emerson joined the Plymouth City Police on 22 April 1950 on transfer from his home force at Gateshead Borough where he served for 20 months from 19 August 1948. Prior to starting his police career he spent almost eight years with the Royal Navy (17.8.39 to 10.5.47), leaving as a leading seaman (No. C/SSX 31140).

He was commended once in Gateshead, on 6 July 1949, by the Chairman of Newcastle City Magistrates in connection with an arrest for the theft of scrap lead from British Railways. During his service in Plymouth he received three further commendations, two from the Magistrates at the City Court and one from the Chief Constable.

In 1952 he was recommended for the award of the George Medal by his Chief Constable - Mr John Skittery - after he had tackled a disturbed man who was armed with a knife on 29 November 1951. On 7 May 1952 he was awarded the British Empire Medal for Gallantry.

In the early hours of Thursday, 29 November 1951, Constable 57 Emerson was sent to an address in Plymouth following a report that a man there had been drugged. As he arrived he found the man concerned standing at the entrance to the house. It very soon became apparent to Constable Emerson that the man was suffering from some form of mental disorder and he tried to persuade him to return to the house. Without warning the man ran off down the street shouting. John Emerson ran after him and caught him after 300 yards or so. As he reached him, the man turned and raised his hand as if to strike the officer. John Emerson put up his hand to ward off the blow and moved his head backwards at the same time. He did not know that the man had armed himself with a knife some 11 inches long and was aiming it at him. As the man's arm came down he caught Constable Emerson on the chin with the blade causing a slight nick.

The man ran off again but Constable Emerson again caught him and managed to subdue and disarm him after a struggle and with the help of a member of the public. The man was arrested. He faced no charges as a result of the incident but was sent to a local psychiatric hospital where he stayed for some time. In addition to the cut to his chin, John Emerson sustained a blow to his left hand and wrist which caused him to report sick for a short while.

John Emerson was well aware of the fact the man was armed with a knife when he chased and tackled him the second time and he was fortunate not to be more severely injured.

John Emerson stayed with the Force for a further five years but resigned on 24 March 1957 to emigrate to Canada. He stayed there for three years before deciding to return to England and, if possible, resume his police career in

Plymouth. He contacted the Chief Constable but was told that it was completely contrary to his policy to re-engage a man once he had left his police force.

The Chief Constable stated that he would have taken him back but for his strict adherence to this policy and, in fact, wrote glowing references to the Commissioner of the Metropolitan Police and the Chief Constable of Bristol City Police when John Emerson applied for appointment to those forces.

John Emerson's Plymouth City personal record gives no indication if he was successful in either application.

William Godfrey Edward MATTHEWS
(Cornwall)

William Matthews joined his local police force as Constable 317 on 16 March 1953, after two years national service with the RAF, and served initially at St Just and Penzance, not far from his home at Gulval (born 21 June 1930). On 28 August 1956 he was seconded to Cyprus as a police sergeant, returning to Wadebridge to resume his career two years later. Whilst stationed at St Just, on 21 December 1954, he was awarded the British Empire Medal for Gallantry for his actions in recovering the body of a man who had fallen over the cliffs. The award is noted in his personal record from the Cornwall Constabulary:

> GO 1/55 para 1 26.1.55 *Awarded BEM for brave conduct at St Just on 9th August 1954 when he descended sheer cliffs to rescue the body of a man who had fallen from cliff top.*

A more detailed account is recorded in the citation published in the *London Gazette* of 21 December 1954:

> *A man was seen lying at the bottom of the Levant cliffs, St. Just. Constable Matthews was informed and immediately went to the scene of the accident. The cliffs at this spot are particularly dangerous, rising vertically to about 120 feet. Matthews descended the cliff by first getting on a narrow ledge, allowing his body to drop over the face of the cliff whilst clinging with his hands and then releasing his hold and dropping on to another ledge about 10 feet below. A false step and he probably would have been killed. He descended this way until he reached the man who unfortunately was found to be dead. A rope ladder was then lowered and the body raised to the cliff top.*

William Matthews was commended twice by his Chief Constable, once in his original force and once in 1983 after the four forces had been amalgamated into the Devon and Cornwall Constabulary in June 1967. As a constable, in 1965, he received a 'Favourable Record' with four other officers for:

> *zeal and initiative in conducting enquiries resulting in the detection of 63 crimes in Camborne and Truro Divisions and the prosecution of 15 persons for offences of warehouse-breaking, office-breaking, canteen-breaking, store-breaking and larceny. Also complimented by Chairman of East Penwith MC on 12.8.65.*

He had a successful police career, being promoted to the rank of chief inspector at Bideford where, on 13 July 1983, he received his second Chief Constable's commendation, again with others, for:

> *skill, initiative and courage in a potentially dangerous situation when, unarmed, they arrested a man armed with a sword and what appeared to be a rifle.*

William Matthews retired on 20 June 1984 after 31 years service.

Spencer Maconochie VIBART
(Plymouth City)

Spencer Vibart joined the Plymouth City Police on 20 May 1946. He was promoted to inspector with that force and served until his retirement from the Devon and Cornwall Constabulary on 31 August 1976. As a constable in Plymouth in 1957 he was awarded the BEM for Gallantry:

Constable Vibart was parading to go off duty at midnight, when a call was received to the effect that a gunsmith's premises had been entered, and a man had been seen running away. The call was immediately attended to by another wireless crew and Constable Vibart left the building to walk to his home. On his way he saw a man acting in a furtive manner endeavouring to conceal something inside his jacket. The constable caught up with the man who suddenly turned, pointed a pistol at the Constable and threatened to shoot him. The Constable had an attaché case in his hand and he threw this at the gunman and at the same time went for him in a rugby tackle. There was what appeared to be a click of the fall of the hammer of the pistol but no report, and a struggle ensued. The man broke away and ran off. Vibart pursued him and caught up with him. He turned and threw the pistol at the Constable but it missed. There was a further struggle and with assistance the man was overcome and arrested. The pistol was found to be unloaded.

(*London Gazette*, 8 October, 1957, page 5818).

Brian FARTHING
(Plymouth City)

Brian Farthing joined his native Salford City Force on 28 November 1957 but transferred to the Plymouth City Police on 5 September 1960. He was promoted to sergeant in that force and received further promotions after the amalgamation in 1967; to inspector on 1 July 1975 and chief inspector on 1 September 1978. He retired as a superintendent from the Devon and Cornwall Constabulary on 22 March 1993. In 1961, as a constable in Plymouth, he was awarded the BEM for Gallantry for the rescue of an elderly man from a house fire in Plymouth:

A fire occurred on the second floor of a small three storey boarding house. Constable Farthing saw smoke billowing through windows and the open front door. He was told that the seat of the fire was in an upstairs room and that there was an elderly man in this room. The Constable immediately went to the top of the house and began a search of each room. On the second floor, he came to a back bedroom, the door of which was closed. He opened it and found the interior of the room a mass of flames and full of smoke. He dashed into the room and saw the outline of a man who was kneeling face downwards on the floor. His clothing had been burnt off and his flesh was on fire. Farthing managed to pull the man out to the landing and attempted to put out the flames. The man was then carried downstairs and taken to hospital.

(*London Gazette*, 31 January 1961, page 764)

William Henry FORD
(Devon)

Sergeant 80 Ford (born on Boxing Day 1916) joined the Devon Constabulary on 1 October 1938 at the age of almost 22. He spent the early years of his service at

Torquay before joining the Armed Forces on 15 October 1942. He returned to the Constabulary on 1 April 1946, going back to Torquay after a short spell at Force Headquarters at Exeter for a refresher course. He stayed there for just over two years before moving to headquarters in July 1948 where he remained until he was promoted to sergeant on 18 June 1955. He moved to Crediton on 6 January 1956.

During his time at Crediton he was awarded the British Empire Medal for Gallantry for:

> *his courage, initiative and devotion to duty during the floods at Crediton during September 1960. Announced in the* London Gazette *of 20.6.61.*

(entry in personal record).

The *London Gazette* entry also notified the award of the BEM to four civilians and the MBE for gallantry to two others:

> *To be Additional Members of the Civil Division of the Most Excellent Order of the British Empire, for Gallantry:*
> *William John Cloke Markby, M.R.C.S., L.R.C.P., General Practitioner, Crediton, Devonshire.*
> *Vincent Paul Trevor Trought, M.R.C.V.S., Veterinary Surgeon, Rochester, Kent.*
>
> *Awarded the British Empire Medal for Gallantry (Civil Division):*
> *Walter John Edwards, Chemist, Exeter, Devonshire.*
> *William Henry Ford, Sergeant, Devon Constabulary.*
> *Michael John Isaac, Baker's Roundsman, Black Torrington, Devonshire.*
> *Alfred Charles Ridholls, Baker's Roundsman, Beaworthy, Devonshire.*
> *Alfred John Wiles, Lorry Driver, Forest Gate, London.*
> *For courage, initiative and devotion to duty during floods in Southern England.*
>
> *The low lying town of Crediton was severely affected by floods and many small houses were rendered uninhabitable. One set of four cottages which partially collapsed contained three elderly women. They were trapped in the upper part of the cottage and were rescued by Dr. Markby and Mr. Trought, who risked injury, and possibly drowning, in their efforts to bring them to safety. Police sergeant Ford was in charge of the flooded area throughout this incident and many others. Mr. Edwards and Mr. Wiles risked injury when effecting the rescue of a boy who was trapped in the entrance of a submerged culvert near Exminster. Mr. Ridholls and Mr. Isaac rescued an elderly man who had been carried away by the flood water near Holsworthy and was in danger of drowning.*

(*London Gazette*, 20 June 1961, page 4575)

The floods which struck Devon in late September 1960 were the worst in living memory. After a night of high winds and rainfall almost tropical in its intensity rivers broke their banks and streams which were little more than a trickle a few weeks earlier brought havoc to the City of Exeter and surrounding towns and villages.

Over the following week some 50 miles of coastline in the south and east of the county and almost every low-lying town or village inland were affected. At Teignmouth, between 10 am on Thursday 29 September and 10 am the next day, some 2.2 inches of rain fell; at Honiton a river flowed where the A30 trunk road should have been and the River Otter which was usually a mere 10 feet wide had grown to 400 yards or more.

The devastation caused was widespread and immense - in Exmouth alone, 600 houses were flooded and roads within a 12 mile radius of Exeter were littered with rubble and debris. Further rain fell over the next few days adding to the chaos and destruction - at Colyton and Axmouth, three inches fell in 90 minutes and Teignmouth recorded the heaviest levels of rainfall for 60 years - more than eight inches in six days.

Crediton was as badly hit as anywhere with severe damage being caused to several houses - so severe that sailors from the Royal Naval Air Station at Yeovilton were drafted in to assist. At one stage it was estimated that 250 troops were sent to Devon.

On 3 October the waters receded allowing cleaning up operations to start in earnest, although Exmouth suffered a second period of flooding on the night of 5/6 October after more heavy rain, and again the following night. It was not until ten days after the rains first came that the county could begin to get back to normal.

Countless small acts of courage took place, many going unrecorded or unnoticed amongst the chaos but the deeds at Crediton were rewarded in the Queen's Birthday Honours List the following June.

Sergeant Ford was first told of the impending crisis on the morning of Friday 30 September 1960 by a lady who was concerned that the River Yeo was rising

Left and below: Flooding at Fordton, near Crediton in 1960.

Above: *Floods in Cowick Street, Exeter and* (right), *in Alphington Street.*

rapidly. By the time he had reached the area some 15 minutes later the river had broken its banks and the road was flooded although, at that stage, there was no undue cause for alarm - local residents told him that their cottages had never been flooded in similar circumstances in the past.

It soon became apparent that the situation was more serious than was first thought and that many houses were under threat. At South View Cottages in the Fordton area the force of water had caused one wall to collapse and trap the three elderly lady occupants. Dr Markby was standing chest deep in the water trying to pacify the ladies until help arrived. By noon, the water had risen to the tops of the doors and a second wall had collapsed - the lives of the stranded ladies were at great risk. Mr Trought was seen standing in the water up to his shoulders trying to find a way into the cottages without success. With the help of Sergeant Ford he managed to force a door against the weight of the water and reach one of the ladies who was disabled. He brought her safely from the cottage and returned to rescue an 83 year old lady who he passed to Sergeant Ford who carried her to safety. The third lady was rescued with the aid of the Fire Brigade.

All the while, Dr Markby walked around the other houses in the area, up to his shoulders in water, consoling other trapped persons until they too could be rescued. He also helped Sergeant Ford rescue one person from a collapsing cottage. There were no casualties during the flooding due to the work of Sergeant Ford and the others.

William Ford was promoted once more during his career on 16 March 1965 and retired on pension as an inspector four years later (30 April 1969) from the Devon and Cornwall Constabulary. He died at Crediton on 3 November 1996.

John Anthony Grant ROBB
(Devon and Cornwall)

The two counties of Devon and Cornwall have always been a popular part of the country for officers whose origins lie elsewhere, a situation more prevalent now with ready access available from all areas and a more mobile population, although all four constituent forces have always been affected to a certain extent.

Many officers joined directly but others transferred to the West Country from other forces - in some areas a true Devonian or Cornishman was something of a rarity and a range of regional accents could be heard in most stations.

John Robb was one such officer - a native of Wimbledon - he joined the Metropolitan Police as a cadet in 1964 and was appointed a constable there on 9 September 1966.

He served with that force in two spells until he transferred to Devon and Cornwall (Constable 560) in 16 April 1976. His service took him to North Devon, Teignmouth and Plymouth before his retirement on 20 March 1996.

During his service in London - on 8 December 1967 - he was commended by the Commissioner of the Metropolitan Police for:

outstanding courage and determination in effecting the rescue of a man from the roof of a building.

He was subsequently awarded the British Empire Medal for Gallantry (*London Gazette* 14 May 1968, page 5455):

A message was received that a man was on the roof of a building and threatening to jump off. Constable Robb immediately went to the building where a man was standing on a narrow ledge around a dome about 90 feet above the ground and shouting that he was going to jump. Robb stepped on to the ledge on the north side of the dome to the right of the man and started talking to him but he moved away and threatened to jump if the officer came any nearer. Robb started to edge towards the man who by that time was on the outermost part of the ledge immediately above some spiked railings. All this time the officer was talking to the man who continuously kept up his threats to jump if he came any nearer. When he saw a turntable ladder was being raised towards him he became very excited, made further threats to jump and when the ladder was half-way up he went limp and fell forward in a dive-like position. Robb immediately stepped towards him and pulled him back towards the dome. The man at first struggled violently and the Constable, while being held by other officers, had to use considerable force to restrain him and keep him on the ledge The man then collapsed and Robb, still supported by the other officers, had to hold him to prevent him falling to the ground. The turntable ladder eventually reached the ledge and the man was lowered to safety.

Gwyn John LLEWELLYN-REES
(Devon and Exeter)

Gwyn Llewellyn-Rees was awarded the British Empire Medal for Gallantry in 1968. He joined the Devon and Exeter Police on 17 June 1966 as Constable 373 and served slightly less than 30 years taking his time as a cadet into account. He retired on 23 March 1996.

As a recruit he was posted to Plymstock but moved to Ilfracombe, North Devon, whilst still a probationer. He stayed in North Devon for the rest of his service apart from a few very brief periods spent away, including an overseas secondment to Rhodesia in February and March 1980 to help supervise the elections there.

He won the BEM as a probationer in Barnstaple on the night of 15 October 1967, the brief circumstances are contained in the Chief Constable's Annual Report for 1968:

> *Constable G J Llewellyn-Rees was awarded the British Empire Medal for Gallantry for his brave conduct on 15th October, 1967, when he ascended the pillar of a crane to a height of 135 feet in total darkness and, in appalling weather conditions, reasoned with a man who had threatened to commit suicide. The constable spent twenty-five minutes at the top of the crane before succeeding in grabbing him and successfully escorting him to the ground.*

Gwyn Llewellyn-Rees was an incident car driver stationed at Ilfracombe who just happened to be at Barnstaple police station with his partner when the call was received from a local doctor reporting that a patient of his had threatened to commit suicide by jumping from a tall building in the town. The call was traced to a kiosk close to the site of the new Civic Centre then under construction in North Walk.

The two officers made a search of the area, initially without any sign of the man, but saw a cigarette glowing at the top of a tower crane on the construction site and the shadowy figure of the man. Attempts to persuade the man to come down by shouting up to him were fruitless; someone would have to climb closer to him to reason with him.

Constable Llewellyn-Rees climbed to the top of the crane, a distance of some 135 feet, and began to talk calmly with the man who was depressed and in a state of shock, as a second officer also began to climb up to join carrying with a rope which they might have had to use if there was any danger of them falling. He managed to persuade the man to come away from his position at the very edge and grabbed hold of him, holding him against the main framework of the crane.

After a little more persuasion, the man agreed to go down and followed Gwyn Llewellyn-Rees to the ground safely. Two other officers, who had by then partially climbed the crane themselves, were able to help by making sure there was no change of mind by the man and a return to the top.

The man received medical treatment and was allowed to return home shortly afterwards. On the night the weather was atrocious with a strong wind and heavy rain.

Gwyn Llewellyn-Rees was recommended for the Chief Constable's Commendation with Star (the Force's highest honour) by his divisional commander but it was decided at Headquarters that the level of courage displayed was worthy of national recognition.

The award of the British Empire Medal for Gallantry was approved by the Home Office and Constable Llewellyn-Rees was invested at Buckingham Palace on 27 February 1968.

Ernest Frederick JONES
Michael Philip BROOME
(Devon and Cornwall)

Sergeant 1354 Ernest Jones and Constable 1058 Michael Broome were awarded the BEM for Gallantry on 18 June 1974 for saving the life of a thirteen-year-old boy who had become stuck on the tidal mud flats at Camels Head Creek, Plymouth.

On the afternoon of Saturday 23 February 1974, Sergeant Jones was called to the flats following a report that a young boy had become stuck in the mud. He saw the boy standing up to his knees in the thick sticky mud some 25 feet from a stream carrying effluent away from the sewage works nearby. The situation made more perilous by the rising tide due to cover the flats very soon.

Ernest Jones tried to cross the mud to reach the boy but also started to sink. He lay on his front and edged his way across to the boy who had by then sunk to his waist. He was told to put his arms into the air enabling Sergeant Jones to pull him out a short way but, as soon as he released his grip, he sank back once more.

Michael Broome arrived shortly after and crawled across to the boy and Sergeant Jones. Together they prevented the boy from sinking completely by supporting his head and speaking to him to calm and reassure him. By the time the Fire Brigade arrived with ladders all three were almost completely submerged in the mud. A ladder was passed across which they managed to place under the boy and lever him out of the mud. This caused them to sink further into the mud themselves until they too were rescued with the aid of the ladder.

There is no doubt that they saved the boy from a particularly unpleasant death and were in severe danger themselves which they faced knowing the possible consequences.

Ernest Frederick Jones joined the Plymouth City Police on 22 September 1952, was promoted to sergeant on 5 October 1971 and retired after 30 years service exactly. He was commended five times by his Chief Constable and his actions in saving life were recognised by the Royal Humane Society on three separate occasions:

(a) In 1960 he was awarded a testimonial on parchment for his prompt action diving into the water at the Barbican and rescuing a 4-year-old girl from drowning and assisting her uncle who had previously tried to save her.

(b) In 1969 he was awarded a resuscitation certificate for successful mouth-to-mouth resuscitation in saving the life of a man who had been found unconscious and bleeding from severe lacerations.

(c) On 20 August 1975 he received a testimonial on vellum for the rescue of a young woman who had threatened to commit suicide by jumping from the Tamar Bridge.

Michael Philip Broome joined the Devon and Cornwall Constabulary on 1 November 1971 and still serves in Plymouth. He has been commended once by the Chief Constable on 23 January 1991 for:

initiative and prompt action in a dangerous situation with another officer. They rescued a suicidal man from the parapet of a multi-storey car park some 70 feet above ground level.

These were the last awards of the BEM for Gallantry made to officers in Devon and Cornwall - it was discontinued the same year.

KING'S AND QUEEN'S POLICE MEDAL FOR GALLANTRY

This is the only gallantry award exclusively for police officers. Instituted in 1909, there was initially no distinction between medals awarded for gallantry and those given for distinguished service, the medal and ribbon being the same. In 1933, the first recognition of the difference was established with the addition of three narrow red stripes on the white of the ribbon to indicate that it was awarded for gallantry.

The following year the reverse of the medal carried an inscription indicating why it was awarded - 'for gallantry' or 'for distinguished service' - the differences in the ribbon being retained. From 1951, the gallantry award has only been awarded posthumously.

Since its inception, 12 officers from the two counties have been awarded the medal for gallantry - nine in Cornwall, two in Devon and one to the current combined Force.

One of the very first police officers to receive the medal (for distinguished service) in the King's Birthday Honours List of 1909 was the Deputy Chief Constable of the Cornwall Constabulary, William Henry Beare, a Devonian from Holsworthy.

He joined the Force on 8 December 1864 at the age of 20 and rose steadily through the ranks until 1 December 1902 when he was appointed Deputy Chief Constable. He retired on 30 September 1910 at the age of 66 years.

The Chief Constable, Major Hugh Protheroe-Smith, recorded the award in his Force Standing Orders published on 1 December 1909:

The Chief Constable has much pleasure in stating that among the list of recipients of the King's Birthday Honours, 1909, His Majesty was pleased to award the Police Medal to William Henry Beare, Deputy Chief Constable of Cornwall. The Chief Constable is glad to take this opportunity on behalf of the Force of congratulating Deputy Chief Constable Beare on the well deserved award bestowed on him which is an honour not only to the Deputy Chief Constable but also to the whole force.

Harry White TURNER
(Cornwall)

Constable 41 Turner was awarded the King's Police Medal for Gallantry in January 1914 for his actions whilst stationed at Padstow on the night of Sunday 12 November 1911.

In a fierce gale off the north Cornish coast an Irish schooner, the *Island Maid*, had run aground on the Doom Bar after suffering damage in the storm and

The Daily Mirror

THE MORNING JOURNAL WITH THE SECOND LARGEST NET SALE

No. 2,514   Registered at the G.P.O. as a Newspaper.   WEDNESDAY, NOVEMBER 15, 1911   One Halfpenny.

WONDERFUL HEROISM DISPLAYED BY CORNISH VOLUNTEER LIFEBOATMEN WHO RESCUED THE CAPTAIN OF A FRENCH SAILING VESSEL.

A noble deed was performed by a volunteer lifeboat crew at Padstow, Cornwall. Two vessels were seen approaching the harbour during a fierce gale, and the crew of the lifeboat Arab was summoned. Residents of Hawkers Cove, where the lifeboat house is situated, quickly got the boat afloat, and the crew, having arrived from Padstow, set out. They rescued the crew of the first vessel, the Island Maid, which struck the dreaded Doom Bar, and brought them ashore. Meanwhile the second vessel, the Angele, of Brest, also struck the bar, but the men after one attempt declared that it was impossible to reach the doomed vessel. Coxswain W. Baker then got together a volunteer crew, who rescued the captain from the rigging. (1) The Arab and its crew. (2) Captain Lazac, of the Angele. (3) The two wrecks: (A) the Angele, (B) the Island Maid. (4) The volunteer crew, which included a police-constable.—(Vaughan T. W. Paul.)

running for the shelter of Padstow harbour. The lifeboat *Arab* was launched and succeeded in reaching the vessel and taking off the crew. As they were making their way back to safety a second vessel, the French brigantine *Angele*, also foundered on the bar. The lifeboat crew safely landed the crew of the *Island Maid* and put out again in an attempt to rescue the crew of the *Angele*.

The storm had intensified by then, however, darkness had fallen and conditions were made considerably more dangerous. Waves were breaking over the vessel causing the crew to take refuge in the rigging as the lifeboat made an attempt to reach them. The crew were exhausted from the previouis rescue and their battle against the wind and sea failed. They returned to the station where the coxswain called for volunteers to make a second attempt. Great difficulty was experienced mustering a crew, however, due to the extreme dangers involved.

Harry Turner volunteered to man the lifeboat himself and succeeded in gathering together sufficient men to make a second attempt at rescue. In spite of the conditions they succeeded in reaching the ship but it had by then been submerged and only the Master (Captain Lazac) was picked safely from the sea, all other crew members were lost. PC Turner's bravery is recorded in his personal record:

> Granted a 'Favourable Record' for bravery displayed in volunteering and going out in the lifeboat in saving life from a vessel in distress near Padstow.

A further entry dated 5 January 1914 notes the fact that he was awarded the King's Police Medal for conspicuous gallantry.

Harry Turner (born 21 October 1883 at Perranzabuloe) joined the Cornwall Constabulary on 24 March 1904 after five years service with the 1st Volunteer Battalion of the Duke of Cornwall's Light Infantry (DCLI). He served in a number of towns and villages in addition to Padstow, including Newlyn, Port Isaac and Chyandowr until his retirement at Hayle on 28 February 1931.

His police career was interrupted by war service with the Military Mounted Police between July 1915 and May 1919 but he returned to Cornwall on his discharge from the Army. His personal record contains one other granting of a 'Favourable Record' on 1 March 1914 for:

> brave conduct at Hayle on 13th February, 1924, when he, at great personal risk, stopped two runaway horses attached to a cart partly laden with sand, (the driver having been killed) thereby preventing the possibility of further loss of life.

Harry Turner continued with a very active life after his retirement from the Police Service, he was a member of the Royal Institution of Cornwall, chairman of the West Cornwall Water Board, West Penwith Rural Council and Hayle Parish Council, an inspector for the Ministry of Food in the Second World War and a bard of the Cornish Gorsedd with the official title of *Gwythas-en-Cres*, 'Guardian of the Peace', in addition to a host of other interests and offices. He founded the Hayle Ambulance Brigade and served as the superintendent for many years.

Harry Turner died suddenly in Hayle, aged 79, in 1963. He is buried at Longstone Cemetery, St Ives. At his funeral the church was packed to capacity with representatives from countless organisations and all walks of life, reflecting the high esteem in which he was held in Cornwall.

Samuel Thomas BISHOP
(Cornwall)

Samuel Bishop (born 28 September 1888 at Camborne) joined his home force on 1 September 1912 and was serving at Liskeard when he attempted to stop a runaway horse and cart on 9 August 1919 in the town. He was unfortunately thrown aside by the impact and suffered a broken skull and other injuries preventing him from resuming duties until well into the new year, and after he had been awarded the medal. He was not fully fit at the time of the accident, still feeling the effects of illness contracted during his war service in France between 14 November 1915 and 3 March 1919.

Samuel Bishop never recovered fully and retired as unfit for further service on 31 January 1924. He settled in Redruth after his retirement.

He was awarded the KPM for Gallantry for his actions, on 1 January 1920. A brief entry in his personal record reads:

Awarded the King's Police Medal for distinguished bravery in stopping a runaway horse at Liskeard on 9th August, 1919.

His conduct was described as 'exemplary' and his ability as 'good' - his record ends with a few words giving the cause of his leaving as 'injuries received on duty'.

William John BROOKING
(Cornwall)

The thought of awarding the KPM for stopping or attempting to stop a runaway horse may bring a smile to the faces of officers more used to danger coming in the form of a knife, gun or other offensive weapon. As the example of Samuel Bishop illustrates, however, the danger is extreme and the courage of the officers honoured should never be underestimated.

The calm behaviour displayed by William Brooking in Redruth on 2 April 1924 conceals the level of courage he needed to stop two horses who had broken free from the traps they were pulling after a collision.

The accident was caused by one horse galloping down Fore Street, pulling a trap, crashing into another at the bottom of the hill. They ran off together towards PC Brooking's traffic control point. He calmly stood in front of the first horse and stopped it before taking hold of the reins of the second to bring it under control. He was pulled some way along the street but managed to hold on and bring the animals to a halt.

For his actions he was awarded the KPM for Gallantry on 1 January 1925. His personal record contains two references to the event:

1.5.1924. Granted a 'Favourable Record' for brave conduct at Redruth on 2nd April, 1924, when he, at great personal risk, stopped two runaway horses, thereby preventing what might have been a serious accident.

followed by an entry in red:

Awarded the King's Police Medal for distinguished bravery in stopping two runaway horses at Redruth on 2nd April 1924. (Ref. No. 453,652 of 31st December, 1924).

John Brooking was a Devonian, born in Loddiswell on 19 October 1888, who joined the Cornwall Constabulary (Constable 18) on 6 October 1913 after eight years service with the DCLI. He was recalled to the colours in August 1914 and served until February 1919. He was wounded during the war but returned to his police career. His service was all in the west of the county at Newquay, Falmouth, Newlyn and Redruth, where he was stationed when he resigned on 30 November 1939.

Charles Young BROWN
(Devon)

Before the current headquarters complex was established at Middlemoor in 1939 the County Force HQ was sited in New North Road in the building now housing the Remand Centre next to the main Exeter Prison. Many areas of the existing City of Exeter were policed by the Devon County Force although in times of emergency the boundary wasn't a barrier to the officers of either force.

On the night of 3 June 1927 a fire was discovered in a refreshment room at what is now Exeter Central Railway Station in Queen Street. Constable 227 Charles Brown, then stationed at Whitstone, was off duty and on the station platform. When he heard that a man was trapped in an upstairs room he ran into the building, up the stairs and searched for him, but found no one. He left the room and made his way to the top of the stairs where he was overcome by heat and smoke and collapsed, falling headlong down the stairs.

Other rescuers managed to pull Charles Brown from the building but he suffered severe burns in his attempt to save the man. He was close to death for several days but recovered to serve a further 18 years with the Force. It was later discovered that the man he sought had made good his escape from the fire over the roof of the station.

The officer's actions were recorded in the Devon Constabulary Order Book, dated 28 June 1927, by Ralph Helford Thompson, Deputy Chief Constable, in a few words:

> *Const. No. 227 Brown, Charles Y. has been highly commended - by the Chief Constable - for his plucky action in endeavouring to save human life at a fire at Queen Street Railway Station on the 3rd instant. The Standing Joint Committee also appreciate his gallant behaviour in the case. The constable was badly burned and had to be removed to hospital.*

On 26 October 1927 when, presumably, he had fully recovered from his injuries and returned to work, his Chief Constable, Captain Herbert Vyvyan, rewarded him in a more tangible fashion;-

> *Constable No. 227 Brown, Charles Y. having passed the examination required for promotion and having continued to perform his duties with zeal, intelligence and proficiency is hereby granted a second special increment of 2/- [10p] weekly = 8/8 [44p] per calendar month on and from 1st Sept. 1927.*

(Force Order Book, page 55, Order No. 24 of 1927)

On 1 January 1928 Constable Brown was awarded the KPM for Gallantry. Later in his service, on 1 October 1935, Charles Brown was awarded a further additional increment of 2/6d [12p] weekly but, some seven months afterwards, fell foul of the discipline code of the times and was saved from dismissal from the Force partly by his actions at the fire and his previous good character. The Order Book entry of the time, dated 27 May 1936, records his sins and punishment:

> *A constable of F Division has been fined three days pay (39/8) [£1.32p] and two days pay (26/5) [£1.89p] respectively and ordered to pay a fee of 10/- [50p] due to an Ambulance Authority, for the following offences, committed on the 25th April, 1936:*

> *(1) Discreditable Conduct - while attending a public dance, being in a condition through drink likely to bring discredit on the reputation of the Force.*

(2)   Drunkenness - while off duty and attending a dance at 1.15 am; he was therefore unfit to take up his tour of duty at 5.30 am on the same date through drink.

I decided neither to dismiss him, nor to call on him to resign for the following reasons;-

(i)   his state of health consequent on an heroic action some years since;

(ii)   that he was off duty when the more serious offence was committed;

(iii)   his truthfulness during the enquiry, and

(iv)   his assurance of future abstention from intoxicants.

Charles Brown joined the Force on 1 September 1920, his stations during his service including Newton Abbot and Tiverton - he retired at Bratton Clovelly on 31 August 1945.

John Samuel WARREN
(Devon)

When it was built in 1806, Dartmoor Prison at Princetown was as isolated as it was possible to get; access was terrible, conditions worse, and the chances of a successful escape not only from the prison itself but also from the Moor were slim. With the good roads and ease of access today, it can be somewhat difficult to imagine how daunting it was to serve a sentence there and why it had acquired its fearsome reputation.

After it had been converted to a convicts' prison in 1850, from its former role as one for prisoners of war (French and American), the level of attempted escapes increased. Early police response was fragmented with no real plans available to mount a proper search for the escapee.

On 2 April 1931, Major Lyndon Henry Morris MC left his post as Governor of the Prison to become the new Chief Constable of the Devon Constabulary. He very soon introduced the first prison escape scheme which remained as Force policy for many years, refined over the years to take account of changing circumstances but the basis nonetheless for the scheme in operation today.

Many escapes were made and, on 12 October 1934, one was to lead to the award of the King's Police Medal for Gallantry to Sergeant 135 John Samuel Warren, then stationed at Moretonhampstead, some 12 miles distant.

The words of the Chief Constable as recorded in the Force Order Book for 20 December 1934 relate most eloquently the circumstances leading to the award:

Sergeant No. 155, Warren, John S., is hereby highly commended for his conspicuous gallantry in effecting the arrest of two desperate convicts named Ernest Collins and Leonard Hollins in Moretonhampstead on the 12th October 1934. These men had escaped from a working party at Dartmoor Prison about half-an-hour earlier. They had then attacked the driver of a motor van with an iron bar, rendering him partly unconscious, and continued their flight in his van. Reaching Moretonhampstead, they were challenged by Sergeant Warren, who had been notified by telephone of their escape and attack, and who, armed only with his truncheon, and alone, with great courage and tenacity, and in the face of attacks with an iron bar and a fire extinguisher, succeeded in detaining them until the arrival, some five minutes later, of four local residents whom his wife had pluckily assembled.
(Order No. 39 of 1934)

Sergeant Warren was awarded his KPM on 1 January 1935:

His Majesty The King has granted the Police Medal to Sergeant No. 135 Warren, John Samuel, of Moretonhampstead, E Division.

(Force Order No 1 of 1935)

John Warren joined the Force on 1 October 1909 at the age of 23 and served initially for almost eight years until 16 April 1918 when he was released to join the Army in the Great War.

He was re-appointed on 17 January 1919 and served until his retirement on 30 September 1935, nine months after the award of his medal.

Charles Percy COLE
(Cornwall)

The circumstances leading to the award of honours to officers of the Cornwall Constabulary often reflect the nature of the county and the times in which they lived. Runaway horses were a relatively common occurrence with a number of officers receiving 'Favourable Records' for stopping them. Others were commended for rescues involving ships in distress or accidents around the coast.

The existence of mine shafts dotting the countryside also played a part in the lives of many Cornish officers with people and animals frequently falling into them.

Constable Cole was awarded the King's Police Medal for Gallantry for his attempt to rescue a boy of eight who had fallen into a disused shaft whilst playing with friends.

PC 143 Cole (born 17 January 1913 at Truro) joined his home force on 1 February 1932 and served at Camborne, Truro and Probus. He won his award whilst stationed at Camborne on 4 September 1937.

A report submitted by his sergeant (Gerald Rogers) quite clearly records the level of bravery displayed by Charles Cole although it understates the dangers involved.

Cornwall Constabulary
Camborne Station

September 21st 1937

Sir,

re: Aubrey Gilbert - Fall into Mine Shaft.

I respectfully report that on the 4th September 1937, at 6-10 p.m. when I arrived at the Police station, Camborne, it was reported to me that the above named, (who had been playing near an old Mine Shaft, at Stray Park, Camborne, with two other boys) had fallen into the shaft.
P.C. Cole, who came on duty at 6 p.m. had received a report from Mr Samuel Bennetts of Moor Street, Camborne, that his nephew, Aubrey Gilbert, had about 15 minutes earlier, fallen into the Shaft, P.C. Cole had gone to the spot.
I immediately went there and on arrival found a large number of people inside the fence and around the top of the shaft, P.C. Cole was there and he had his tunic off, in readiness to descend the shaft. On seeing what arrangements were made, I offered to go down, but he declined.
I made some enquiries on the spot and gathered that the two other boys, Garnet Gilbert and Raymond Edwards, both of Moor Street, Camborne, last saw Aubrey

Gilbert standing at the mouth of the shaft in the act of throwing a bicycle frame down, when he suddenly disappeared, they looked around the outside and found he had gone and immediately reported it to Mr Samuel Bennetts; fresh marks at the mouth of the shaft, indicated that something had gone down.

The depth of this shaft was then unknown and the bottom was not clearly discernible. It was known that an Adit came into the shaft several feet down and it was thought that the boy may have been on a ledge some distance down the shaft, lying injured.

Planks of wood had been secured from Mr. W. Donald, of Stray Park, Camborne; lengths of rope had also been obtained from him and Mr. E.T. Sara, Railway Foundry, Camborne; Mr. Lawry of Carnarthen St, Camborne and Cornwall Electric Power Company, Camborne.

Four lengths of rope were joined together by Mr Norman Williams, Stray Park; & Mr. Percy Heath, Carnarthen St. Camborne. Three planks were then placed across the top of the shaft.

P.C. Cole was then secured to one end of the rope, in a 'Bo'suns Cradle' and lowered into the shaft, the rope sliding over the side of the planks, the other end of the rope being held by a large number of helpers.

The extent of the rope was reached, when it was found that he was still some considerable distance from the water; an additional length of rope was secured and attached and he was lowered further down, but it was still found that he was some considerable distance from the water, although the length of rope was about one hundred feet.

There were no more suitable lengths of rope available, and no more immediately obtainable and in view of the time he was suspended in the shaft, his legs became numbed and I decided to have him hauled up; from the time he descended until he ascended, was about 25 to 30 minutes.

A new rope was then obtained from Messrs Tyacks (1926) Limited, of Church Street, Camborne; P.C. Cole was again secured in a similar was to this rope and was then lowered to the waters edge; from this position he made a thorough search of the Shaft, but there were no signs of the Boy; he used an electric torch while down the shaft.

The second descent took about 15 to 20 minutes and it was found that the length of rope used was 176 feet.

After this was done, there appeared to be no chance of recovering the Boy alive and the search was abandoned.

Your obedient Servant,
Gerald Rogers
Sergt

Supt. Hosking
Camborne.

A letter written after the tragedy to the Chief Constable by a mining engineer from South Crofty Limited at Carn Brae spelt out the dangers faced by PC Cole. He described how the mine shaft had not been used for almost 100 years and was in very poor condition. The timbers at the top had decayed, the walls were in danger of collapsing into the shaft if they were disturbed too much during the rescue and, in common with all old mines, there was the additional, invisible, danger of accumulations of noxious gases which would very quickly be lethal in the confined space of the shaft. Charles Cole's efforts were rewarded by the granting of the King's Police Medal in the New Year's Honours List published on 1 January 1938.

The Investiture was held at Buckingham Palace on 15 February when the officer was presented with his medal by King George VI, noted briefly in his personal record on 15 February 1938:

Awarded the King's Police Medal for that he on the 4.9.37, at great personal risk and in the face of unknown danger twice descended the East Shaft of the Camborne Vean Sett at Stray Park, Camborne, in a gallant attempt to rescue a boy aged 8 who had fallen into the shaft.

Attempts were later made by professional miners and others to recover the boy's body. One of these attempts ended in a further tragedy and the death of a civilian - the body was never found.

Charles Cole was promoted to sergeant on 1 October 1944 and transferred to Truro. He was further promoted to inspector on 1 November 1952 and retired at Bude on 6 May 1965.

Horace OSBORN
George Edgar APPLETON,
Leslie John Stanley JONES
Noel Heatley WILKINSON
(Cornwall)

The position of the County of Cornwall in the British Isles has meant that shipwrecks and reports of vessels in difficulties were regular occurrences. On the night of 31 January 1938, the wreck of the steamship SS *Alba* was to lead to the award of the KPM for Gallantry to four officers, the highest number ever awarded in the south-west for a single event.

The weather and sea conditions on 31 January 1938 were as bad as anyone could remember, a strong north-west gale was blowing, the seas were high, rain and hail were pouring down and it was pitch black. The SS *Alba* was driven ashore on to the rocks at Porthmeor Beach on the Island at St Ives with the stern stuck fast and heavy seas breaking over her

The St Ives lifeboat was launched and safely made her way to the lee side of the *Alba* although she was battered by waves the whole time. The 23 Hungarian crew members of the *Alba* were taken on board the lifeboat which then prepared to draw away. She backed out of the shelter into the heavy seas and was hit broadside almost immediately by a huge wave, capsizing her. The engine was drowned and could not be restarted causing the lifeboat to drift inshore where she was eventually thrown on to the rocks.

The lifeboat crew and those rescued from the *Alba* were pitched into the sea. The four officers together with several colleagues, coastguards, fishermen and members of the public then set about pulling them ashore. In all 18 of the *Alba's* crew and all the lifeboatmen were rescued.

There were a number of individual acts of bravery and the words of the officers concerned in their reports following the rescue barely do justice to their courage:

A few minutes later a man was observed about 50 yards out to sea from the rocks. I discarded my uniform with the exception of shirt and trousers and made an attempt to get to the man by jumping on to the rocks seaward, which were practically under water. I managed to get within about 15 yards of the man, when a huge breaker broke right over me and I was thrown about in the sea against the rocks.
I managed to get on to another rock, and again located the man, who then appeared to be further out to sea, but another breaker washed him in closer, to within about 8 yards of me. I dived into the sea, got to the man and grabbed him; he also grabbed me and we both went under the water and parted when another huge breaker broke over us, and I was again thrown helpless against the rocks. When the sea abated a little I managed to hold on to a rock and found I was much closer to the Island as also was the man.

I again held the man and was assisted by many willing helpers in bringing the man to the Island rocks, and I then cut his neck lifebelt and loosened clothing around the man's neck. Ambulance men were there and I left them in charge of him. This man, I later learned was the Donkeyman, who is now at St Ives Hospital.

(Leslie J S Jones).

The funeral of crew members of the SS Alba, the stricken vessel still lying offshore at Porthmeor, St Ives.

The rescued man, Donkeyman Yene Gersitz, survived. A donkeyman on a ship was a crew member with special responsibilities in the engine room, most likely he was in charge of the ship's donkey engine, a small auxiliary engine

I immediately clambered over the rocks to the sea where men were being swept about. On seeing a man floating in the sea out past the rocks, I attempted to swim out to him, but was washed back onto the rocks by a big wave.
After a number of attempts I managed to get hold of the man, but instead of being able to swim back with him I was carried out to sea further, eventually being washed against some rocks; on feeling myself being pulled out to sea again, I fell, together with the man between some rocks from where we were assisted by many helpers; this man had injuries to his thigh, and I have since ascertained that this man was the captain.

(George E Appleton).

Captain Horvath survived. Statements made by witnesses at the scene and letters later received by the Chief Constable gave further evidence of the officers' courage:

P.C. Jones, in trousers and shirt... worked unceasingly, in driving rain on the rocks, to bring back to life two senseless men by artificial respiration, and his efforts were crowned with success.

(A W Delaney- Priest in Charge, Catholic Church)

It seemed as if anyone was washed on the rocks they would be smashed to pulp before they could be rescued. I brought my torch which is a powerful one, with me, and I was amazed to see P.C. Jones had stripped off his uniform and with only shirt and trousers on - enter the sea to recover a body. I kept the beam of my torch on him and saw him swept off his feet and go under, coming to the surface again he made another attempt to make contact with the body and succeeded but the body had life in it and clutched P.C. Jones like a drowning man will, they both disappeared again and when they came up they had separated, again Jones tackled him and successfully brought him to the helpers on the rocks.

A wave knocked P.C. Appleton over like a cork and then engulfed him, rising he made another attempt and was again beaten by the waves, his next attempt succeeded and Appleton after a terrible struggle gained the rocks exhausted.

(George S Parker)

Officers Osborn, Appleton, Jones and Wilksinson outside Buckingham Palace after the investiture of the King's Police Medal for Gallantry.

For their courage, each officer was awarded the King's Police Medal for Gallantry on 2 January 1939. Their personal records each carry an entry recording the award:

14.2.39. Awarded the King's Police Medal for conspicuous gallantry when the steamship 'Alba' was wrecked off the Island, St. Ives on the night of 31st January, 1938.

The bravery of three of the officers involved was recognised by His Serene Highness the Regent of the Kingdom of Hungary with the award of the Gold Cross of Merit to Horace Osborn, and the Silver Cross of Merit to Constables Appleton and Jones. The four officers received these awards, at what was to have been a public ceremony, at Curnow's Café, St Ives on 4 February 1939, led by the local Member of Parliament. However, the Coxswain of the St Ives lifeboat, who had also been awarded the Gold Cross, had tragically lost his life in a second disaster at sea and the ceremony was kept a private affair out of respect for his memory.

A fifth officer, Constable 200 John Tomkin James, was nominated by the Chief Constable together with the others but the then Home secretary declined to submit his name to the King.

The senior officer at the scene, Horace Osborn, had twice before been granted 'Favourable Records' for bravery in 1929 for:

1.8.29 brave conduct at Pole Hill Quay, St. Agnes on 21st June 1929, when at great personal risk, he descended a disused mine shaft and rescued a dog which had fallen in.

1.10.29 for descending a very dangerous mine shaft on Aug 8th 1929, at Blue Hills, St Agnes, and rescuing an Alsation dog which had been there for several days, but was still alive.

For this second rescue he was also awarded a Silver Medal and Bar by the RSPCA.

Born in Bodmin on 22 May 1899, Horace Osborn joined the Cornwall Constabulary, as Constable 122, on 1 September 1920 and served at Falmouth, Camelford and St Agnes when he was promoted to sergeant and moved to Lewannick on 1 December 1931. Further promotions followed but he sadly died in service at Liskeard, where he was superintendent, on 2 November 1952, aged 53.

The careers of all four officers were cut short, none managing to serve through to normal retirement on pension.

Noel Wilkinson, a native of Saltash, born on 20 December 1913, served for less than nine years. He joined on 20 October 1936 (Constable 40), serving at Camborne, St Ives, Constantine and Helston before resigning on 31 August 1945 for reasons which are not recorded.

George Appleton (Constable 214) joined on 1 December 1930. He served at Camborne, Redruth, St Ives and Veryan but died suddenly, at the age of 27 years, on 5 December 1939 from a thrombosis. He left a widow and two children.

His service record contains little more than brief details of the award of his medal, his stations and one disciplinary matter. On 27 February 1933 he appeared before the Chief Constable on two charges of: (1) neglect of duty and (2) falsehood or prevarication. He was fined £1 and cautioned as to his future conduct.

Leslie Jones - a Devonian from Holsworthy (born 2 March 1911) - served for 17 years and, initially, had a promising career before him. He joined on 1 January 1930 (Constable 233) and was promoted to sergeant on 1 January 1946. On 17 May 1947, however, he appeared before his Chief Constable on two charges of discreditable conduct and was reduced to the rank of constable with effect from the following day.

He also suffered a financial penalty by being placed on the ten year rate of pay (132/- [£6.60p] per week). On 2 June 1947, he was removed from Launceston where he had served as a sergeant to Lanivet as a constable. He resigned on 12 July 1947.

Arthur Enos DAVIES
(Cornwall)

For a period, the KPM was renamed the King's Police and Fire Services Medal for Gallantry and awarded to officers from both bodies until a separate award was created for the Fire Service. Arthur Davies won his medal on 23 July 1948 for the rescue of a drowning man from the sea at Widemouth Bay near Bude.

The award was notified in the *London Gazette* of 11 March 1949 and in his personal record:

> *Awarded King's Police Medal for Gallantry at Widemouth Bay, Poundstock on 23.7.48.*

On the afternoon of Friday, 23 July 1948, James Black, a holidaymaker from Staffordshire, found himself in difficulties bathing in the sea off Widemouth Bay, near Bude. When he realised he was having trouble he relaxed and floated thinking that the tide would carry him back to the shore. Unfortunately, due to the strong undercurrents, he drifted out to sea and was some 400 yards offshore when Arthur Davies started his rescue attempt. Attempts had been made by others but they found they were unable to reach Mr Black.

PC Davies tied a lifeline around his waist and swam out towards the man in trouble. He managed to reach him and started back towards land but the currents carried them amongst rocks. With the aid of a chain of helpers on the beach, PC Davies succeeded in getting Mr Black to safety.

Arthur Davies was in the water for almost 45 minutes and suffered cuts to his legs as they hit the rocks. He also suffered shock and exposure as a result of the rescue and was off work for a short time afterwards.

Mr Black made a full and speedy recovery and wrote to the Chief Constable the following day to express his thanks and offer a small gift of appreciation to Arthur Davies.

24th July, 1948

Dear Sir,

In addition to the formal statement given P.C.Robb, I wish to express my appreciation of Constable Davies' courageous action in going to my rescue yesterday afternoon. If it is proposed to recommend him for a Life-Saving Award, I would be happy to give it my full backing.

While I understand it is not the custom of the Constabulary to permit their officers to receive gifts I ask you in this instance, Sir, to make an exception, and permit me to send a small present for you to pass to Mr Davies.

I am, Sir,
Yours sincerely
J. K. L. Black.

Major Hare agreed, in the special circumstances, to allow Arthur Davies to accept the gift provided that it wasn't 'a monetary one'. Two weeks later a watch arrived and was presented to the constable. It was not the first gift he had been permitted to accept from a grateful person. His personal record contains one other commendation of a 'Favourable Record' awarded on 30 December 1935 for:

> *brave conduct at Launceston on 8th December 1935, when he, at great personal risk, ascended a ladder and rescued a woman who was kneeling on the window sill in a state of acute delirium.*

Sadly the lady died later in hospital but her family presented Arthur Davies with a gold watch, again with Major Hare's permission, in appreciation of his efforts to save her.

The giving of a small token to a police officer was not uncommon in the pre-war years, particularly in circumstances where a life was saved or the officer had placed his own life at risk. The gift often took the form of a suitable inscribed watch, usually silver but, on occasions, gold.

Arthur Davies came from Glamorgan and joined the Cornwall Constabulary on 1 July 1933. He served at a number of towns and villages across the county including Bodmin, Delabole, Jacobstow, Fowey and Egloskerry. He was promoted to sergeant on 1 March 1955 and retired on pension at St Austell on 31 August 1963.

Dennis Arthur SMITH
(Devon and Cornwall)

Dennis Smith is the only officer from Devon and Cornwall to have been the recipient of the QPM for Gallantry. The award was only given posthumously. He was murdered in Torquay at the age of 44 (born 7 November 1929) a few days before Christmas 1973 by one Martin Fenton who was later convicted of four murders and sentenced to life imprisonment - he died behind bars in 1995.

The citation taken from the *London Gazette* dated 18 March 1975, when the award was notified, gives only the briefest of detail but shows how routine, everyday police work enacted countless times a day by officers everywhere can lead to tragedy:

> *Constable Smith who was on panda patrol in Torquay (on 21 December 1973) radioed that he was chasing a car whose driver (a man named Fenton) appeared to be drunk. In subsequent radio messages he said he had stopped the car and arrested the driver and asked for assistance. Exactly what happened will never be known, but it appears that Constable Smith detained the driver and removed the keys of his car, but the driver then succeeded in escaping back to his car where he had a loaded pistol. Then it was heard that Constable Smith in attempting to reason with the man, was shot at very close range in the chest. The man fired two more shots at point blank range while Constable Smith lay on the ground and then drove off in the police car. Constable Smith died shortly afterwards. Constable Smith's courage and devotion to duty were in the highest traditions of the police service.*

The citation does not say that Fenton went to a nearby night club where he shot and killed three other people and wounded two more before driving off away from Torbay in the stolen police car. He abandoned the panda car and took a second vehicle, driving off towards Exeter.

In the hunt that followed he was seen driving the stolen van near Exeter and pursued at high speed into the countryside away from the city. He was stopped at Newton Poppleford and arrested by two officers from Exeter and one from Sidmouth, all themselves displaying great courage considering what he had done. Fenton had two loaded pistols beside him in the van as the unarmed officers approached. He was also suffering from self-inflicted knife wounds

Dennis joined the Devon Constabulary on 21 June 1965 after service with the Metropolitan Police (5 May 1950 to 9 July 1961). He served as a patrol constable and with the Traffic Department at Newton Abbot before his transfer to Torquay.

KING'S AND QUEEN'S COMMENDATION FOR BRAVE CONDUCT

First awarded in 1939 during the reign of King George VI as the King's Commendation, it takes the form of a small silver laurel leaf which is worn alone on the tunic on the left breast where any medal ribbon is usually worn. A holder who is also entitled to wear the Defence Medal for services during the Second World War wears the insignia on the ribbon of that medal.

The silver insignia is only awarded to civilians, including police officers, and never to members of the Armed Forces. Any service personnel recommended for the award are entitled to wear the oakleaf signifying a Mention in Despatches on the appropriate medal ribbon.

A number of officers of the combined Force and the constituent forces, including the Special Constabularies, have received the King's or Queen's Commendation for Brave Conduct.

Frederick John BALSOM
(Plymouth City Special Constabulary)

The first King's Commendation awarded to a police officer in the West Country went to a member of the Special Constabulary. Special Constable Balsom was one of the original members of the Special Constabulary Mobile Section formed to support the regular force traffic department to provide an efficient transport system during the air raids.

The section worked continuously during the raids and, on 18 July 1941, Frederick Balsom was awarded the King's Commendation 'for brave conduct in Civil Defence:' he drove throughout the air attacks for long periods in support of regular officers with a total disregard for his own safety. When interviewed following the announcement of the award he modestly accepted it on behalf of all his colleagues.

William John LORAM
(Plymouth City)

William Loram joined his local force on 6 October 1927 after almost three years service with the Coldstream Guards. He served for 29 years, retiring on 7 July 1957 with the rank of inspector. As a sergeant, on 25 July 1941, during the Blitz on Plymouth, he was awarded the King's Commendation for Brave Conduct:

> *At the City Hospital, Plymouth, which had received a direct hit by a HE bomb during an intensive air attack.*

In the early years of his service, on 24 April 1930, together with another officer, he was commended by the Watch Committee in circumstances which would today be considered somewhat unusual:

On the night of the 8th March, whilst off duty, Constables Loram, No. 36 and Francis, No. 117, found at Devonport Hill an attaché case, containing Bank notes to the value of £220.3.8, which they at once took to Ker Street Station. The Watch Committee warmly commended the two Constables for their honesty. The Committee also stated that, whilst they expected the highest standard of honesty from the members of the Force, they felt that there was in this case considerable temptation and that the action of the Constables concerned would enhance in the eyes of the public the standard of police honesty and integrity.

The money found represented almost a year's salary to the two officers.

George Henry STRATHON
(Plymouth City Special Constabulary)

George Strathon was an inspector in the Special Constabulary when he was awarded the King's Commendation for Brave Conduct on 10 April 1942 for his actions during the Blitz of March 1941.

On the day of the air attack which led to his award he had been on duty for many hours in connection with the visit to Plymouth of the King and Queen. He was at his home when the alert sounded but before he was able to report to his station in Morice Street, incendiary bombs fell around his home area.

He took charge of the operations to deal with the fires caused and was partially successful in putting out a number of incendiaries. The second wave of attackers, however, dropped high explosive bombs causing damage to houses with people buried beneath rubble and some fatalities.

He gathered together a group to start rescue work and was primarily responsible for saving the lives of three women and five men who were trapped in the wreckage of their houses. He remained on duty all night and until 10 am the following day, assisting with rescue work and manning a hose to fight fires with the attack continuing the whole time and high explosive bombs falling.

George Strathon was well known in Plymouth through his work as a motor engineer and for his interest in amateur dramatics in which he was a singer of some repute.

Ernest FRASER
(Exeter City)

Constable 56 Fraser joined the Exeter City Police on 1 June 1927 after three years' service with the Royal Artillery. A native of County Durham (born 19 October 1902), he served for 30 years, retiring on pension with the rank of inspector on 27 July 1957.

He was awarded the King's Commendation for Brave Conduct on 7 October 1942 for his actions during the Blitz on Exeter:

Commended by HM the King for his gallant conduct on 4th May 1942 when despite falling masonry he effectively rescued three people from a shelter at 3 East Avenue. Reported to the Watch Committee on 26.11.42.

Ernest Fraser was twice commended by his Chief Constable in the course of his police service:

29.1.29 for zealous conduct in the arrest of a shopbreaker on the night of 19th January 1929.5.3.30

Scenes of devastation in Exeter. These photographs show the damage caused by bombing in Paris Street where firefighters are still at work dousing the flames.

Above: *Cathedral Close, Exeter.
An air raid warden surveys the
damage after the night's bombing.*

Right: *An Exeter family save what
little they can from the wreckage of
their home in Prospect Park.*

Frank Naughton GC

George Cross, 1939-45 Star, Burma Star, Defence Medal, War Medal, Coronation Medal, Jubilee Medal, Police Long Service and Good Conduct Medal.

OBE (Military Division).

George Medal (Richard Willis).

MBE (Civil Division).

British Empire Medal and Plymouth
City Police Good Conduct Medal
with Gallantry Bar (John Lindsey).

British Empire Medal
(Daniel Crutchley).

King's Police Medal for Gallantry
(Charles Brown).

RSPCA Silver Medal
(Richard Hardy).

Distinguished Conduct Medal, Military Medal and Bar 1914-15 Star, War Medal, Victory Medal and Defence Medal
(Richard Hardy).

166 Squadron Crest.

Exeter City Police Long
Service Medal.

Croix de Guerre (France).

Military Cross.

Distinguished Flying Cross and Bar, Queen's Police Medal for Distinguished Service 1939-45 Star, Air Crew Europe Star with France and Germany Bar, Defence Medal, War Medal and Police Long Service and Good Conduct Medal (Arthur McCartney).

Arthur McCartney DFC. QPM taken in 1977.

Forged butter ration coupons dropped over Berlin on 1 April 1944.

John Evans DSO at Susteren.

Distinguished Service Order.

Distinguished Flying Cross.

Forged ration coupon – 'a gift from the Führer.'

INSTRUCTIONS

(1) Learn by heart the Russian phrase "Ya Anglicháhnin" (*means "I am English" and is pronounced as spelt*).

(2) Carry this folder and contents in left breast pocket.

(3) If you have time before contact with Russian troops, take out the folder and attach it (*flag side outwards*) to front of pocket.

(4) When spotted by Russian troops put up your hands holding the flag in one of them and call out the phrase "Ya Anglicháhnin."

(5) If you are spotted before taking action as at para 3 do **NOT** attempt to extract folder or flag. Put up your hands and call out phrase "Ya Anglicháhnin". The folder will be found when you are searched.

(6) You must understand that these recognition aids **CANNOT** be accepted by Soviet troops as proof of bona fides as they may be copied by the enemy. They should however protect you until you are cross questioned by competent officers.

Я англичанин

"Ya Anglicháhnin" (*Pronounced as spelt*)

Пожалуйста сообщите сведения обо мне в Британскую Военную Миссию в Москве

Please communicate my particulars to British Military Mission Moscow.

Part of the escape kit carried by air crew likely to come into contact with the Red Army.

Distinguished Service Cross – a mystery.

George Cross

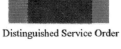

Distinguished Service Order

Order of the British Empire
(Military Division)

Order of the British Empire
(Civil Division)

Distinguished Service Cross

Military Cross

Distinguished Flying Cross

Distinguished Conduct Medal

George Medal

King's and Queen's Police Medal
for Gallantry

Military Medal

Distinguished Flying Medal

Queen's South Africa Medal

King's South Africa Medal

India General Service Medal

1914 Star

1914 - 1918 War Medal

Victory Medal

1939 - 1945 Star

Atlantic Star

Air Crew Europe Star

Africa Star

Pacific Star

Burma Star

Italy Star

France and Germany Star

Defence Medal

1939 - 1945 War Medal

Meritorious Service Medal

Croix de Guerre
(France)

Croce di Guerra
(Italy)

Order of St George
(Imperial Russia)

for zeal and efficiency of observation which led to the arrest of a man named Hawkins for larceny.

In addition he was commended three times by the Watch Committee:

> 6.12.34 *(with PS Kelly and PC Noble) for courageous attempt at the rescue of a woman at a fire on 12/11/34. Also highly praised by City Coroner at inquest.*

> 3.12.36 *for astuteness and attention to duty in effecting the arrest of a man wanted at Chippenham for stealing money from telephone boxes.*

> 13.7.39 *for his action in effecting the arrest of a man wanted in many police districts for theft and fraud, on 17.6.39.*

The three officers involved in the attempted rescue of the woman from the fire in November 1934 were also awarded the Bronze Medal of the Society for the Protection of Life from Fire (19.2.35).

Clarke Edmund TROTT
(Devon)

Clarke Trott was awarded the Queen's Commendation for Brave Conduct for the leading part he played in the rescue of a youth from a precarious position on a crumbling cliff at Sidmouth on 28 July 1953.

PC 113 Trott (born 6 September 1911 at Kingsnympton) joined the Devon Constabulary on 1 October 1934. He served at a number of towns including Dartmouth, Bampton, Torquay and Ottery St Mary before he was promoted to sergeant, the rank he held when he received his award, on 1 July 1941. He was further promoted to inspector on 1 September 1956 and finally to chief inspector at Exmouth five years later. He retired on 31 December 1965.

Three years before he received his award he was commended by the Chief Constable (27 September 1950) for:

> *with Const No 452 STONE and No. 397 HAYES for bringing a long and difficult case of theft of foodstuffs & breaches of the Feeding Stuffs (Rationing) Order 1949 to a successful conclusion. They also received the congratulations of the Magistrates when the case was brought to court.*

Bertrand BRIDGE
(Devon)

Constable No. 427 Bridge was born in Brixham on 28 July 1915 and joined the Coldstream Guards as a young man. The disciplined life, high moral code and camaraderie were much to his liking and led directly to his decision to join the Lancashire Constabulary on 2 July 1937.

After war broke out he rejoined the Army on 1 December 1939 and served as a member of the Guards Armoured Division in Western Europe. He was Mentioned in Despatches for courage displayed at the battle of Nijmegen Bridge in the Netherlands.

He left the Army on 6 October 1945 and returned to Lancashire to resume his police career. On 1 June 1948 he transferred to his home force in Devon and served until he retired at Exmouth on 1 July 1967.

He stayed as a member of the support staff at Force Headquarters, Middlemoor until he finally retired, aged 65, in 1980.

In 1954 whilst stationed at Exmouth he was awarded the Queen's Commendation for Brave Conduct for his part in the attempted rescue of an engineer who had been overcome by fumes as he was carrying out an inspection of a sewer under The Parade, Exmouth. Bertrand Bridge was himself overcome by the gases and rescued by a member of the community who was also honoured. He needed hospital treatment for several days and almost died from the ill effects of the gas inhaled.

Bertrand Bridge's war service medals including the oakleaf signifying the Mention in Despatches, his Police Long Service and Good Conduct Medal and Queen's Commendation laurel leaf are on display at Exmouth police station.

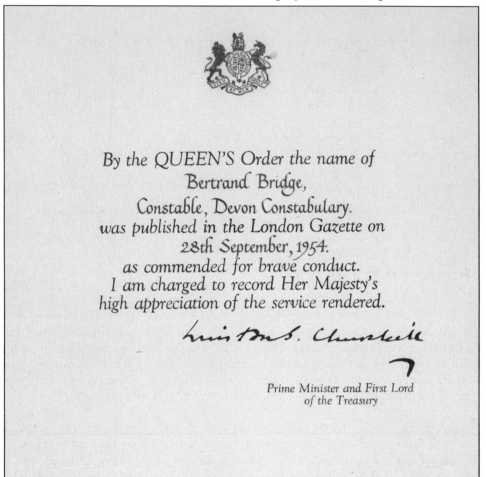

By the QUEEN'S Order the name of
Bertrand Bridge,
Constable, Devon Constabulary.
was published in the London Gazette on
28th September, 1954.
as commended for brave conduct.
I am charged to record Her Majesty's
high appreciation of the service rendered.

*Prime Minister and First Lord
of the Treasury*

Frederick John Michael WHITE
(Cornwall)

Born in Penryn, Cornwall on 29 September 1922, Frederick White joined his home force on 21 February 1947 (Constable 69) after war service with the Royal Air Force from 1 October 1940 to 8 April 1946. In his first spell of police service, which lasted barely eight months, he was stationed at Looe, St Cleer and Bude until 4 November 1957 when he was seconded to Cyprus as a police sergeant for two years.

He returned to Cornwall and served further at Bude and Falmouth until his retirement on pension on 11 March 1973 from the Devon and Cornwall Constabulary.

In 1957 he was awarded the Queen's Commendation for Brave Conduct following his arrest of an armed and dangerous criminal who he had disturbed in the act of breaking into a garage in the early hours of the morning .

He was on patrol alone at the time, with no help immediately available and likely to be some time arriving had he been able to summon it, but managed to subdue the man after an extremely violent struggle in which he was very lucky not to be seriously injured. The circumstances are noted in his personal record:

GO 6/57 27.6.57 (para 10)   Granted a 'Favourable Record' for his initiative and tenacity of purpose displayed in effecting the arrest of James Stanley Wheatley ROBINSON CRO 31495737 at Bude at 2.30 am on 15/5/57 for garagebreaking. At Manchester Assizes on 5/6/57 Robinson was sentenced to 10 years PD. Judge Sir Basil Neild commended the Constable's courage and determination in arresting a very dangerous criminal.

The Judge publicly applauded Frederick White's courage and determination in the face of:

a violent attack on a police officer with a weapon which, if it had struck him on the head, would have killed him.

A second entry in his record, dated 24 October 1957, notes the award of the commendation:

Awarded Queen's Commendation for brave conduct in connection with the above.

Reginald John HAWKINS
Bertram Roy PEARN
(Cornwall)

Both officers were awarded the Queen's Commendation for Brave Conduct on 24 October 1957 and were also honoured by the inclusion of their names on the roll of heroes of the Carnegie Hero Fund Trust, the only known occasion on which this honour has been bestowed upon police officers from either of the two counties, noted by an entry in the personal records of both officers:

GO 6/57 27.6.57. Carnegie Hero Fund Trust decided to have the names of Sgt B R Pearn and PC 285 Hawkins inscribed on their illuminated roll of heroes in recognition of heroism on 21/3/57 when they rescued Mr S J Besley from a savage attack by a bull. Awarded the Carnegie Hero Fund Trust Honorary Certificate framed in oak.

The farmer, Samuel Besley, aged 42, went into his field at Common Moor, Liskeard to turn out two moorland ponies which had strayed in from the moor. Mr Besley had some difficulty driving them out and whilst his attention was distracted by the ponies, he was attacked by his bull. Mrs Besley witnessed the attack and called the police.

The two officers saw the bull and six heifers surrounding Mr Besley who was lying on the ground in obvious pain. They succeeded in enticing the bull away and Sergeant Pearn was able to keep it away from Mr Besley with a shovel whilst Constable Hawkins gave first aid to the injured farmer.

Mr Besley's father, a man of 82 years, then arrived on the opposite side of the field and managed to attract the bull's attention away from Sergeant Pearn. As the bull began to approach him, Mr Besley senior shot it with his shotgun - he caused little injury but enraged the animal further

Sergeant Pearn ran across to assist Constable Hawkins but the bull once again turned his attentions to them and began to run towards them. The two officers picked up the injured farmer and succeeded in getting him out of the field before the bull could attack again. Mr Besley unfortunately, however, had suffered a severe laceration to his neck from the bull's horns in the attack and died very shortly afterwards.

The Carnegie Trust was established in the early years of the twentieth century to recognise acts of heroism performed by people who risked their lives to save others. It is named in honour of its founder and benefactor, Andrew Carnegie, who was born in Dunfermline, Scotland in 1835. He emigrated to the United States at the age of 13 in 1848 and amassed a huge fortune as the leader of the expansion of the American steel industry in the late nineteenth century.

When he retired he devoted his life to philanthropic activities and it is estimated that he donated $62 million in trusts and foundations in the UK alone with a further $288 million going to similar causes in the United States. The two officers' actions were later recognised again:

GO 11/57 24.10.57. Awarded the Queen's Commendation for brave conduct in connection with the above.

Sergeant 229 Pearn joined the Cornwall Constabulary on 1 June 1935 and served for 32 years. He was a local man, born at Polruan on 29 December 1912, and served in most areas of the Force including Truro, Torpoint, Liskeard, Camborne, Tregony and Cremyll. He was first promoted to sergeant (clerk) on 1 September 1950 and posted to Liskeard and again to inspector (clerk) 14 years later at Truro.

His police career was interrupted by Army service in the Second World War between 1939 and 1946.

He retired on pension on 31 May 1967, one week before the Cornwall Constabulary ceased to exist as a separate force.

Reginald Hawkins began his police career with the Metropolitan Police on 28 March 1949 after three years' military service with the Army and transferred to the Cornwall Constabulary on 10 March 1952.

He served at Truro, St Columb Major, Newquay and St Cleer until 4 November 1957 when he was seconded to Cyprus as a police sergeant for two years, returning to Newquay on 7 September 1959. Notification of the award of the Commendation came after PC Hawkins had been seconded to Cyprus.

The presentation to him and Frederick White was made at a ceremony at Government House, an event recorded by Corporal Kenneth Brown of the Royal Army Service Corps and relayed to the Chief Constable of Cornwall:

Cornish Policemen Honoured
in Cyprus Presentation

His Excellency The Governor of Cyprus Sir Hugh Foot G.C.M.G., K.C.V.O., O.B.E., held an open-air presentation of Honours and Awards at Government House on Wednesday, 12th March.
A red carpet was laid from the House to a dais on the lawn. Lined on three sides by white arched balconies and open at the southern end to a view stretching across the clear plains to the distant Troodos Mountains, the setting under a warm Cyprus sky was perfect for the splendour of the ceremony.
The band of the Cyprus Police Force played softly from the shade of trees as Government officials, representatives of the Security Forces, families and friends seated themselves around the lawn and along the balconies.
Trumpeters of the Royal Leicestershire Regiment, their blue and gold uniforms reflected in the garden pool, heralded His Excellency's appearance on the dais.
Resplendent in Colonial dress with white plume, sword and purple sash and accompanied by his Private Secretary, Military Assistant and Aides de Camp, he began the presentation.

From among the forty-three recipients of honours, Sir Hugh had special words of congratulation for the two fellow Cornishmen, Police Sergeants Reginald Hawkins and Frederick White, who received the Queen's Commendation for Brave Conduct.

Sergeant White was for five years a constable in St Cleer, Cornwall, where Sir Hugh played when a boy. Sergeant Hawkins, though not a true Cornishman, belongs to the Cornwall Constabulary. At his own request, Sir Hugh was photographed with them after the ceremony.

When His Excellency had left the dais to join Lady Foot on the Balcony, the skirling of bagpipes was heard and onto the lawn marched the Pipes and Drums of the 1st Bn The Argyll and Sutherland Highlanders.

With the regimental banners dancing in the breeze, the rich green of kilts, the sparkling of jewels and the nimbleness of the sword dance - the Highlanders made a stirring climax to the ceremony.

Kenneth Brown
(Cpl. RASC)

The year of 1957 proved to be an eventful 12 months for Constable Hawkins, in addition to the award of the commendation, the certificate from the Carnegie Trust and secondment to Cyprus, he also faced a disciplinary hearing on 22 February. He was, however, found 'not guilty' on two charges of neglect of duty.

Reginald Hawkins resigned from the Cornwall Constabulary but rejoined the Metropolitan Police a year later.

Robson UNDERWOOD
(Devon)

Constable 626 Underwood was a native of Plymouth who joined the Devon Constabulary on 1 June 1956 six months after he ended his spell of National Service with the Royal Military Police. He served for 25 years and retired on 31 December 1984 with the rank of chief inspector.

He received the Queen's Commendation for Brave Conduct in 1963 - the circumstances are recorded in the Chief Constable's Annual Report for that year:

Her Majesty the Queen was graciously pleased to award her commendation to Constable 626 R Underwood for the courage he displayed in affecting the arrest on the 10th May, 1963 of Vincent King, an armed man wanted for interview in connection with the deaths of four persons in Kent.

Robert Jeremy SWEET
(Devon and Cornwall)

Constable 975 Sweet joined the Force on 12 February 1968 and was initially stationed at Newton Abbot. On the evening of 12 August 1969 he was travelling to start night duty at Newton Abbot from his home at Okehampton when he noticed a vehicle parked by the roadside near Moretonhampstead.

Although there was nothing amiss at the time, it was parked in a somewhat unusual position and he made a mental note of the registration number to check further. These checks revealed nothing of interest and he thought no more about the car as he completed his tour of duty.

At the end of his tour of duty, at about 6.15 am, on his way home, he saw another car bearing the same number as the one seen nine hours earlier parked a short distance away, and stopped to investigate.

As he questioned the driver, ammonia was squirted in his face and he was attacked and beaten with a pair of bolt croppers. He tried to detain the man but was too severely injured. He did, however, manage to reach a telephone kiosk and call for help. The offender abandoned the car and managed to evade the cordon set up after the call for help was received.

When the car was searched officers found explosives, detonators, shotgun cartridges and a holster for a sawn-off shotgun, but no weapon.

A major incident was set up and enquiries led subsequently to the West Midlands where the offender was identified and later arrested in Birmingham and returned to the West Country. He appeared in due course at Devon Assizes and was sentenced to seven years' imprisonment on a long list of charges, including the assault on Bob Sweet.

Constable Sweet spent six days in hospital but fully recovered from his injuries and, in February, he was awarded the Queen's Commendation for Brave Conduct.

On 31 October 1976 Bob Sweet transferred to West Mercia.

Reginald William GOLDSWORTHY
Michael KIVELL
Leslie Harold THORNTON
(Devon and Cornwall)

The three officers were awarded the Queen's Commendation for their actions in Bideford on Monday, 12 March 1973 when dealing with a man armed with a shotgun.

In the early hours of the morning, PC Kivell went to Torrington Street, Bideford following the report of a gunshot. He found a man standing in the street armed with the double-barrelled shotgun which he aimed at the officer whilst he was still in the police car and threatened to shoot him if he came any closer. Mike Kivell left his car and tried to soothe the man. He was told that he would only speak to another officer whom he knew, Detective Constable Leslie Thornton, also stationed at Bideford.

When DC Thornton was called to the scene it was discovered that the gunman was outside the house of a girlfriend and her family - the officers could see that they were all in grave danger. As they tried to reason with him, he repeatedly threatened them and aimed the shotgun at people watching from nearby houses. From time to time he held the gun to his chin, threatening to shoot himself. For more than an hour the two constables and Superintendent Goldsworthy, who had joined them, attempted to reason with him.

It was a bitterly cold night and he was wearing only light clothes causing him to shake violently. There was a constant danger than the gun would be fired accidentally, quite apart from the threats.

The officers managed to get within eight feet of the man and thought they had succeeded in calming him. In a final effort to persuade him to hand over the weapon they agreed to move back a few paces but, as they did so, he shot himself in the head.

The courage of the three officers in the face of very real danger was recognised by the award of the Queen's Commendation for Brave Conduct.

Reginald William Goldsworthy joined the Plymouth City Police on 8 September 1947 and had reached the rank of chief inspector when the amalgamation took place in 1967. He was further promoted in the combined Force and retired as a chief superintendent.

Michael Kivell, Constable 193, joined the Devon Constabulary on 30 September 1955 and retired on pension after 25 years service on 31 December 1980.

Leslie Harold Thornton (Detective Constable 827) initially served with the Derbyshire Constabulary from May 1955 until 14 October 1965 when he transferred to the Devon and Exeter Constabulary.

He resigned from the service on 9 February 1974 'to take up more lucrative employment' after a total of almost 19 years service.

Hedley Langham ROGERS
(Devon and Cornwall)

Constable 2045 Rogers joined the Devon and Cornwall Constabulary on 29 December 1969 after service as a cadet. He left on 31 July 1981. He was awarded the Queen's Commendation for Brave Conduct on 22 April 1975 when he endeavoured to persuade a demented man to hand over a loaded shotgun and for assisting to overpower him whilst still in possession of a gun.

Cyril John EDWARDS
(Devon and Cornwall)

Chief Inspector Edwards was awarded his Queen's Commendation for Brave Conduct in 1976 for his actions at an incident in Bideford on 11 August that year after a man armed with a shotgun had barricaded himself inside a public house in the town.

Cyril Edwards joined the Devon Constabulary as Constable 557 on 28 March 1952 following nine years service with the Royal Air Force from 31 August 1943 until 30 April 1952. He was promoted to sergeant on 25 April 1962 and to inspector on 10 August 1967. His final promotion to chief inspector came on 1 May 1969.

In the first ten years of his service he served at Brixham, Lympstone and Torquay and was commended thirteen times by the Chief Constable and once by the Justices at Brixham Magistrates' Court. The commendations were given for good police work, attention to duty and detective ability, with one exception. In June 1961 following severe flooding in Lympstone, East Devon, in the autumn of the previous year he was:

> *Commended by the Chief Constable for the part he played following the flooding of Lympstone in the Autumn of 1960. The villagers were organised by this Officer and under his direction the work of reclamation and general drying out was performed in a short time, also use of sand bags and boards when further threats of floods occurred. Numerous letters received by the C.C. in appreciation of his efforts.*

He was recommended for the award of the Queen's Police Medal by the Chief Constable - Lieut Colonel Bacon. The Home Office, however, declined to put his name forward for the QPM or any other form of national recognition for his conduct which covered a period of nine days in the autumn of 1960 when large parts of Devon were hit by severe flooding. The extent of the flooding went beyond the county and the Home Office received a large number of recommendations from many quarters. Only the most conspicuous acts of bravery were rewarded nationally although local recognition was made. The Chief Constable's citation paints a clearer picture of Cyril Edwards' actions:

> *Constable Edwards is the sole police officer at Lympstone, a village of some 1,400 inhabitants about three miles from Exmouth. Throughout the period of the flooding in Devon all police in this area were strained to the utmost in dealing with the problems created by the floods and telephone communications were almost wholly disrupted.*
> *Constable Edwards took charge of the situation at Lympstone, arranged for water pumps, for a supply of disinfectant on account of sewage trouble, and enlisted the*

Right: *The Royal Oak is marooned during floods in Okehampton Street, Exeter in 1960.*

Below: *Crowds survey the flood-waters at the junction of Cowick Street and Alphington Street, St Thomas in 1960.*

aid of the Royal Marine camp nearby as well as that of the Women's Royal Voluntary Service and Sea Scouts. The villagers were organised by this officer and, under his direction, the work of reclamation and general drying out was performed in a remarkably short time. When threats of further flooding occurred, he organised the use of boards and sand bags throughout that part of the village which was menaced. Some 106 houses and 13 other premises were all affected by water to a greater or less degree.

*The thatched church of
St Andrews at Exton was
destroyed in the floods of 1960.*

*Subsequently, I received a large number of letters from the inhabitants of
Lympstone, including one signed by nine families, which made it evident that
over a spell of nine days the officer never spared himself in his efforts to protect
the village and to reduce the hardships and discomfort of the inhabitants by his
foresight and leadership.*

*This is an example of a determined man who accepted the responsibility of doing
all in his power to safeguard his people from danger and harm. I have pleasure
in awarding him my commendation.*

Cyril Edwards retired on 27 March 1977.

Jack Stanley SHEPHERD
(Devon and Cornwall)

Often there will be some time between an act of bravery and the award of any
form of national recognition for the officer concerned. Usually it will be several
months later but, in the case of Jack Shepherd, it ran to years. The incident for
which he received the Queen's Commendation for Brave Conduct took place in
Tavistock on Wednesday 8 November 1978, but he had been retired for more
than a year when the award was made on 8 October 1980.

Jack Shepherd joined the Devon Constabulary in September 1949 as
Constable 356, the first step in a successful career which was to see him retire
with the rank of chief superintendent on 27 May 1979 as the Divisional
Commander of the Plympton Division.

Early in his career he served at Totnes, Kennford, Torquay and Bovey Tracey
and earned commendations from the Chief Constable on many occasions, the
first coming whilst a probationer with seven months service on 17 April 1950 for:

his alertness when off duty in arresting an abscondee from Farringdon House.

Others followed regularly until his keenness, hard work and all round ability
were recognised by his promotion to sergeant on 24 May 1962. This was
followed four years later by the rank of inspector on 3 July 1966 and chief inspector 13 months later on 7 August 1967. Three years later, almost to the day, he
was made superintendent 2nd class, and elevated to 1st class on 15 June 1972.

At 2 am on 8 November 1978, as the Commander of the Plympton Division, he was called to an incident at Tavistock Cottage Hospital where an man armed with a stolen shotgun and rifle was terrifying staff and patients after running amok in the town, firing several shots from the weapons, leaving behind him a trail of destruction and a great deal of fear.

He had fired a shot over the head of a police officer, smashed the windscreen of two police cars with the butt of the shotgun and threatened to shoot the officers. By the time he entered the hospital he had fired 24 shots from the shotgun. Jack Shepherd was aware of this when he arrived to take charge of the incident.

Once inside the hospital, the gunman demanded to know where the drugs cabinet was and, when told, shot the door off its hinges. The nurses and 20 elderly patients were subjected to a terrifying 50 minute ordeal by this man.

Jack Shepherd and another officer, dog handler Constable 1348 Graham Ernest Mabbutt, went into the hospital and found the gunman, Brandon John Cooper (22 years) of Plymouth, with a nurse who was trying to calm him.

Cooper demanded the two officers provide him with a car to take him to London, Jack Shepherd agreed to the demand and persuaded him to leave the hospital on this pretext. They left the ward with the gun pointed at Graham Mabbutt's back.

At the main entrance to the hospital he saw the armed police officers who had been called to the scene and threatened to shoot Jack Shepherd if they approached him.

Volunteers to drive the car to London were asked for and two constables, Stephen Pounder and Peter Duffy, came forward. Peter Duffy prepared to drive whilst Stephen Pounder took a seat in the rear of the car. As Cooper approached the car he was surprised to find the officer in the back seat and dropped the rifle as he jumped back. Jack Shepherd grabbed the shotgun and wrestled with Cooper, finally disarming and overpowering him with the help of other officers.

Cooper was sentenced to five years imprisonment at Exeter Crown Court in June 1979.

The four officers involved were each commended by the Chief Constable and, on 3 October 1980, the supplement to the *London Gazette* announced the award of the Queen's Commendation to Jack Shepherd:

> *for services in overpowering and arresting a man armed with a stolen shotgun who had gained admittance into a hospital, stolen drugs and threatened the nursing staff.*

After passing sentence, His Honour Mr Justice Ackner, the Judge at the trial, paid tribute to the actions of everyone concerned. He specifically commended Chief Superintendent Jack Shepherd and the bravery of Edna Blackoe, the nurse who was talking to the gunman Cooper, trying to calm him when Jack Shepherd and Graham Mabbutt first entered the hospital.

On his retirement Jack Shepherd ran the Golden Fleece at Holsworthy before finally opting for the quiet life in North Cornwall.

THE GREAT WAR
1914 – 1918

The carnage that was the 'War to end all Wars' had its effect on officers from the police forces which then existed in the two counties. Many joined up and served in France, Flanders and the other theatres of war - many, like Richard Hardy, came home but thousands died there.

Records available within the current Force are scant and those that do exist usually contain little reference to an officer's actions whilst he was away - often they hold no more than a reference to the fact he left to join the Army and later rejoined - or didn't. More detailed information can be found but will usually only give a tantalising glimpse of events that deserve to be better known.

In the stalemate of the Western Front in France and Flanders, where long periods of attack and counter-attack took place against solid if not impregnable defences, casualties were staggering. The losses touched every family in the land in a way that no war before or since has done. The part played by police officers who joined the Armed Forces cannot be overlooked and any history of policing in the West Country would be incomplete without a reference to them.

The life of Percival Ellis, Constable 48 of the Exeter City Police, is summed up in eight words in his record of police service apart from his personal details. He received no commendations, never fell foul of the stringent discipline of the times, in fact his record is blank for the period of his service from the day he joined on 10 October 1912 to 6 April 1918, except for two entries:

5.8.14. Rejoined regiment.
6.4.18. Died from wounds received in action.

The cause of his leaving is simply stated:

Killed in action.

No. 48	Name	Percival Ellis
	Occupation	6 Co. Army Service Corps Reservist
	Date of Birth	25th February 1892
	Place of Birth	Upton Pyne
	Date of joining the Force	10th October 1912
	Date of leaving	6 apl 1918 Cause of leaving Killed in action
	Height	5'9½"
	Chest Measurement	38" inches

5-8-1914	Rejoined Regiment
6-4-1918	Died from wounds received in action

Constable Ellis was serving with the 16th Battalion of the Cheshire Regiment (Corporal 51356) in April 1918; he is buried in the Namps-au-Val British War Cemetery near Amiens, France.

Wilfred Hammond, Constable 24, was born in Tenbury, Worcestershire on 3 October 1890 and joined the Exeter City Police on 6 October 1913 after serving with the Royal Field Artillery for six years from the age of 17 (150th Battery, RFA, Bombardier 47456). His police service amounted to a mere 211 days before he was recalled to his Regiment (35th Battery) on 5 August 1914. During this time he was commended once by his Chief Constable, on 3 February 1914, for stopping a runaway horse.

On 22 June 1915 he was Mentioned in Despatches by Field Marshall Sir John French for gallant and distinguished service in the Field. A Mention in Despatches is rewarded with a bronze oakleaf emblem worn, in the case of the Great War, on the ribbon of the Victory Medal. Awards made during the Second World War are worn on the ribbon of the War Medal.

On 25 August the same year he was awarded the Medal of St George (2nd Class) by the Emperor of Russia again for distinguished service in the Field. What he did to earn these two awards is not recorded. As a foreign award the Medal of St George could only be accepted and worn with the permission of the

King but, in the war years, this was rarely, if ever, refused. The award was abolished along with all other Imperial decorations, orders and medals in December 1917 after the October Revolution in Russia.

His force record ends with an entry dated 9 September 1917:

Official intimation :- Killed in action in France on 27 Aug 1917.

A letter sent to his wife by his commanding officer, Major Jenkins, was typical of the time:

I should like to send you this small message of sympathy in your recent sad bereavement. Your husband, who was with me once before, and rejoined me again recently, was always one of the very best, and a more reliable, conscientious, and willing fellow, I have never met. He was killed instantly in his gun pit beside the gun, and we buried him near St Eloi. I feel his death personally very much indeed, and all ranks join with me in sending you this message, trusting that you and yours may be sustained in this sad and trying time.

The death of PC Hammond was notified to the Watch Committee in the Chief Constable's Annual Report for 1917 and his colleagues told by way of General Order No 138, dated 21 September 1917:

CASUALTY

Notification has been received of the death of P.C. Wilfred Hammond who as a reservist of the Royal Field Artillery was serving with his Battery in France. The Chief Constable takes this opportunity to express the general regret of all ranks at the loss of this officer who has laid down his life in the service of his country.

Wilfred Hammond is buried at Bus House Cemetery in Belgium, two miles south of Ieper (Ypres) town centre.

Walter James Clarke was killed in action (aged 28) on 11 July 1915 serving with the 1st Devons at Ieper. He is buried at Chester Farm Cemetery just outside the town. Constable Clarke joined the Exeter City Police on 6 October 1913 - the same day as Wilfred Hammond - after seven years service with the 2nd Devons (L/Cpl

8000). As a reservist he was recalled to the Colours at the outbreak of war on 5 August 1914. A local man, he was born at Awliscombe, Honiton on 6 November 1886. He left a widow and two children.

The fate of officers who left Exeter City but who survived and returned to the Force was mixed. Many had suffered wounds which were to affect their careers and, although they were able to rejoin, they failed to serve through to pension.

Alexander William Riggs was another officer from the intake of 6 October 1913 (PC 60) who subsequently went off to war less than a year later. Unlike Walter Clarke and Wilfred Hammond, however, he survived and returned to the Force. In common with many other officers he had previously served with the Armed Forces, in his case with the Highland Light Infantry, 1st Battalion, and was a reservist (No. 9417) when he joined the Police Service. He was recalled to the Colours on 5 August 1914.

On 24 January 1916 he was discharged from the Army as unfit due to injuries received in action but returned to Exeter City albeit on the sick list. He resumed duty in February 1917 having been certified as physically fit by the police surgeon.

His second spell of police service was short but he managed to receive one commendation from the Chief Constable for stopping a runaway horse (14.7.17) and one reprimand and caution on 29 August the same year for:

neglect of duty in failing to report particulars of an accident.

On 5 December 1917 he was:

certified medically unfit for police duty in consequence of injuries received whilst on active service with the HLI.

and resigned.

Robert Thomas Joseph Townhill, Constable 36, left the Force on 5 August 1914 to rejoin his Regiment, the Royal Field Artillery, after five months police service (joined 2 March 1914). During his war service, in October 1914, he was Mentioned in Despatches by Field Marshall Sir John French for bravery in the Field (subject of an entry in the Chief Constable's Annual Report of 1914).

He resigned from the Police Service without returning to resume his career following his discharge from the Army on medical grounds after contracting dysentery and malaria on active service overseas. What happened to him is not known.

Many officers from the Devon County Constabulary also left the Force to serve with the Armed Forces in the Great War - eleven were killed in action or died from wounds they received.

Constable 232 George Sanders (born 24.11.1894) joined the Force at the age of 19 years on 1 August 1914, four days before war broke out but resigned to join the Army on 17 February 1916 and saw service in France and Flanders as Corporal DMA/162524, GHQ Reserve Mechanical Transport Company, RASC.

He was killed in action in France on 4 November 1918 - one week before the Armistice which ended the slaughter. He was the youngest Devon officer to die, three weeks short of his 24th birthday. He is buried at Awoingt British Cemetery, France.

The death rate in the Great War was, at times, almost unbelievable - so high in some instances that whole battalions were almost completely wiped out and regiments affected to such an extent that they ceased to exist as a viable fighting force. The life expectancy of soldiers during the periods of attack and counter-

attack across the swamps and killing fields that were the Somme and Ieper could be short.

Herbert Slader Palmer had served for seven years with the 1st King's Dragoon Guards before he joined the Constabulary on 1 May 1913 (Constable 417) but was recalled to the Colours on the day war was declared on 5 August 1914 - Lance Corporal 6276, 5th Dragoon Guards.

He was sent overseas with the British Expeditionary Force almost immediately but reported killed in action at the Front two months later on 31 October 1914. Herbert Palmer's body was never found. He was one of the 55 000 men who died at Ieper who have no known grave and who are remembered on the Menin Gate in the town.

Walter Gordon, Constable 291, another officer with previous military experience was also recalled on the first day of the war. He had served with the Constabulary since 1 April 1905 after three years spent with the 3rd Battalion, Coldstream Guards - Lance Corporal 4569.

Four months after his return to the Army on 5 August 1914 he was killed by a shell on the last day of the year. He is buried at Le Touret Military Cemetery in the Pas de Calais, France.

When it became obvious that the war would not be over by Christmas a massive recruiting campaign was started and former members of the Territorial Army were called up to replace the regular soldiers lost in the early battles.

Constable 342 Frederick Thomas Dunscombe had two years' experience with the Devon Territorials when he joined the Constabulary on 1 April 1913. He resigned to join the Army two years later (Lance Corporal 23697, 1st Battalion,

Waist-deep mud added to the appalling conditions faced by men fighting on the Western Front.

The Menin Gate, Ieper, Belgium.

Grenadier Guards) and served until the last year of the War. He died from wounds received in action on 29 May 1918 and was buried at Doullens Communal Cemetery, France.

Samuel Feltham Sharp, Constable 29, was another former territorial. He resigned from the Force on 6 June 1915 after five years service (joined 1 May 1910). He enlisted in the 12th Battalion, Gloucestershire Regiment (Pte 20233) but died from wounds received - on 9 May 1917. He lies in Aubigny Communal Cemetery, France.

Two officers from the same intake of seven recruits on 1 January 1914 died after resigning the Force to join the Army.

Constable 58 William Berry joined the Constabulary at the age of 22 (born 5.7.1892) but answered the calls to enlist and resigned on 30 June 1915 - Pte 95420, 2nd Battalion, Royal Fusiliers. He died from wounds five weeks before the Armistice on 4 October 1918 and lies buried in Haringhe (Bandaghem) Military Cemetery near Ieper.

George Augustus Minter Miners (Constable 252), a few months older than William Berry (born 27.4.1892), left the Force on 28 November 1915. He enlisted in the 18th Battalion of the Northumberland Fusiliers (Lance-Serjeant 45367) but was killed in action on 3 April 1917, just over three weeks away from his 25th birthday. He lies in the Ste Catherine British Cemetery in the Pas de Calais.

Frederick Greenslade (PC 257) had served for almost three years with the Royal 1st Devon Yeomanry when he joined the Constabulary on 1 May 1913. He was not immediately recalled to the Colours in 1914 but resigned the Force at the end of 1915 (3 November) to serve with the Army in France - Lance Corporal 2848, Military Police Corps. He died from wounds there on 29 April 1916 and lies in St Sever Cemetery, Rouen.

The war cut short the lives and careers of three other officers from the Devon Constabulary:

Constable 234 John Hawkins, born 1 February 1890, joined up on 27 February 1912 (Serjeant 75621, 244th Siege Battery, Royal Garrison Artillery) but was killed in action on 16 December 1917. His body was returned to Devon and he now lies in Pinhoe (St Michael) Churchyard.

Constable 425 Sidney John Hosgood, born on 22 February 1894, joined the 7th Battalion, Somerset Light Infantry (Pte 20258) on 1 April 1914. He was killed

in action in the battle of the Somme on 16 September 1916 but his body was never found. He is remembered on the Thiepval Memorial.

Constable 324 Lewis Samuel Sparkes, a man from Tedburn St Mary (born 26 September 1893) enlisted on 1 July 1914 (Lance Corporal P/2675, Military Police Corps) but was killed in action on 24 June 1916. He is buried in Cape Town (Constantia) Public Cemetery, South Africa.

All are remembered on a brass memorial plaque at the current Force Headquarters:

from nature's chain whatever link we strike, tenth or tenth thousand breaks the chain alike.

The Cornwall Constabulary suffered in almost equal measure, losing seven officers in the conflict of the 96 who were recalled or enlisted, many very young, with their police careers barely under way. Two other officers died of their wounds after returning to the Force.

William John Sloman joined the Force (PC 196) at the age of 18 on 9 September 1914. After seven months service, on 30 April 1915, he left to join the Army. He died from wounds received in France in 1916, aged only 20, possibly the youngest officer from any of the police forces in Devon or Cornwall to lose his life.

Constable 81 Charles Leonard Webb was a reservist, aged 23, when he joined the Constabulary on 1 December 1913. He was recalled to the Colours at the outbreak of the war but died whilst a prisoner-of-war in Germany.

Two other reservists were similarly recalled in August 1914: PC 88 Samuel Charles Rowe served with the Duke of Cornwall's Light Infantry (1st Bn - Pte

Haringhe (Bandaghem) Military Cemetery, Flanders - resting place of William Berry.

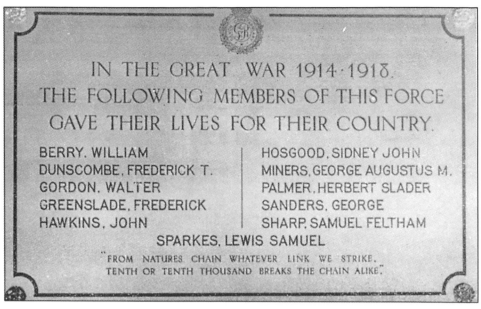

IN THE GREAT WAR 1914·1918.
THE FOLLOWING MEMBERS OF THIS FORCE
GAVE THEIR LIVES FOR THEIR COUNTRY.

BERRY, WILLIAM   HOSGOOD, SIDNEY JOHN
DUNSCOMBE, FREDERICK T.   MINERS, GEORGE AUGUSTUS M.
GORDON, WALTER   PALMER, HERBERT SLADER
GREENSLADE, FREDERICK   SANDERS, GEORGE
HAWKINS, JOHN   SHARP, SAMUEL FELTHAM
                SPARKES, LEWIS SAMUEL
"FROM NATURES CHAIN WHATEVER LINK WE STRIKE.
TENTH OR TENTH THOUSAND BREAKS THE CHAIN ALIKE."

9911) but was killed in action on the Somme on 1 August 1916. He is buried in Dantzig Alley British Cemetery there. PC 211 Walter Gray, aged 24, was also recalled but killed in action in 1916. There are no further details known.

The Force lost two other young men and one more experienced officer: Constable 201 Frederick John Bray, joined the Force on 1 April 1913, aged 18 years, and enlisted on 9 January 1916 (Gunner 137897, 173rd Siege Battery, RGA). He died of wounds on 3 May 1917 - he was 22 - and is buried at Etaples Military Cemetery a few miles from Le Touquet in the Pas de Calais.

Constable 198 Samuel Tom, joined the Force when he was 20 on 21 January 1913, enlisted in the Army on 12 December 1915 (Sjt 137924, 260th Siege Battery, RGA) but was killed in action in 1917 - remembered at Outtersteene Communal Cemetery, Bailleul, France.

Constable 26 Herbert John Luke had served with the Constabulary since 17 April 1909 and been promoted to 2nd class constable exactly three years later. He left to enlist in the Army on 31 May 1915 (Pte P/1522, XV Corps CMP) - he died from wounds received in action three years later on 13 April 1918 - he was 31. He is buried at Lapugnoy Military Cemetery in the Pas de Calais, France.

An 8-inch howitzer in action in Flanders.

Richard S HARDY
(Devon)

Richard Hardy, born in London on 23 March 1896, may have been the most decorated constable to serve in the Devon Constabulary. He joined the Force shortly after the Great War on 1 June 1919 and served a few months less than 30 years, retiring at Lapford on 31 March 1949.

During the War he served as a private (No. 14737) with the Devonshire Regiment before transferring to the 1st Battalion of the Dorsets (No. 14284) - he was discharged with the rank of corporal.

Whilst with the Dorsets he was three times decorated for bravery. He won the Military Medal on 25 April 1918. The award appeared in the *London Gazette* of that date:

> *His Majesty the King has been graciously pleased to approve the award of the Military Medal for bravery in the Field to: 14284 Pte (L./C.) R. S. Hardy, Dorset. R. ([E] Dorset).*

The Military Medal was instituted in 1916 and awarded to non-commissioned officers and men of the Army for bravery. The medal is cast in silver and carries the legend 'for bravery in the field' on the reverse. More than 115 000 awards were made in the Great War and holders are entitled to use the initials MM after their name.

Subsequent acts of bravery which merited the award of the Military Medal were recognised by the granting of a Bar to be worn on the ribbon of the original medal. In the Great War, about 5800 first bars were awarded. The award of the MM ceased in 1993.

On 21 January 1919 the *London Gazette* gave details of the award of a Bar to Richard Hardy's Military Medal:

> *His Majesty the KING has been graciously pleased to approve the award of a Bar to the Military Medal to the undermentioned Non-Commissioned Officers and Men:-*
>
> *14284 Pte. R. S. Hardy, M.M., 1st Bn., Dorset R. (Torquay).*

On 2 December 1919, six months after he had joined the Devon Constabulary, he was awarded the Distinguished Conduct Medal for an act of courage performed on 3 October 1918, five weeks before the Armistice. The *London Gazette* carried a citation:

> *For conspicuous gallantry and devotion to duty on 3rd October, 1918, at Sequehart. He went through the village under intense enemy bombardment, bandaging the wounded and removing them to places of safety. Later in the day he went out in front of our outpost line searching for an officer and a corporal reported as lying in front of our line wounded. He found the corporal and another man and brought them into safety.*

One of the oldest British gallantry awards, dating from 1854, the Distinguished Conduct Medal was first awarded in recognition of distinguished, gallant and good conduct in the Crimean War and is a superior award to the Military Medal. It hangs from a crimson ribbon with a central navy-blue stripe and holders are entitled to use the initials DCM after their name. It was the equivalent of the DSO awarded to officers for similar acts of courage but was abolished in October 1993. During the First World War over 25 000 DCMs were won by Army NCOs and men.

The war left its mark on Richard Hardy; for many years after he was to suffer the effects of what he had seen and done. On 11 April 1927 - almost nine years after the Armistice - he was ordered to Roehampton Hospital by the military authorities for treatment for 'neurasthenia and after-war injuries' - he stayed for 25 days but returned to the Force to continue his career.

Mr John Chanter, the first Devon and Cornwall Welfare Officer, knew Richard Hardy as a pensioner and described him as:

a God fearing man who was proud of the fact that he received his medals for saving life, never for taking it.

On 7 June 1927, Constable Hardy was chosen by the Chief Constable, Captain Vyvyan, to represent the Force at a ceremony performed in Exeter and attended by the Prince of Wales. This honour was most likely a recognition of his standing as the Force's most decorated officer. An entry in the Force Order Book dated 28 June 1927 records the occasion:

Const. 393 Hardy Richard S. as representing the Devon Constabulary was presented to H.R.H. The Prince of Wales at the laying of the foundation stone of the University of the South West of England, at Exeter on the 7th instant. I am sure such privilege and honour will be highly appreciated by every member of the Force.

Later in his service, PC Hardy served at Chelston, Torquay, where he again displayed his courage and compassion when he was awarded the RSPCA Silver Medal on 28 September 1931 for 'descending a deep well to rescue a cat from a recess'. The medal is inscribed 'for animal life saving' and is suspended from a bar with the legend 'For Humanity', a fitting epitaph for a remarkable man.

William ROUNSLEY
(Exeter City)

William Rounsley was born in Exeter on 22 December 1890 and joined his local city force, as Constable 9, at the age of 21 on 10 October 1912 after serving for 3 years with the Army Service Corps.

In 1914 he left to rejoin the Corps and served throughout the war until he was demobbed on 9 June 1919 (Cpl S/28052 GHQ, 3rd Ech (Rouen). He rejoined the Exeter City Force and served until his death on 29 June 1939 at the Royal Devon and Exeter Hospital following surgery.

He was twice commended during the war - in January 1917 he was Mentioned in Despatches by Field Marshall Sir Douglas Haig for devotion to duty (notified to his colleagues in the Chief Constable's General Order No. 24, dated 23 February 1917).

On 18 January 1919 (*London Gazette* page 1009), he was awarded the Meritorious Service Medal for devotion to duty and in recognition of valuable services in France. The Meritorious Service Medal ranks as one of the longest-standing awards in the British Army. First instituted in December 1845 for the Army and later extended to the Royal Marines (1849), the criteria for its award have changed several times since.

Until the Great War it was awarded to selected long-serving warrant officers and NCOs for particularly meritorious service, and was a rare medal. Major changes in the criteria took place in 1916 and 1917 to reflect the changing circumstances of warfare and the vast numbers of men who became involved in the first truly global conflict.

The MSM could be awarded for devotion to duty under war conditions and acts of gallantry in war, other than in action against the enemy, in addition to the original criteria of long and meritorious service. It remains an unusual award still not frequently given.

During his police service William Rounsley was commended once by the Watch Committee (1 May 1913) for:

courageous conduct in securing an infuriated bull which had got out of the control of its drovers on the 9th April 1913.

and twice by his Chief Constable - the first coming on 27 November 1913 for:

prompt and efficient action at a fire at Messrs Bodley Bros premises, Commercial Road.

followed five months later, on 23 April 1914, by another for:

his conduct in the collection of evidence in cases of fortune telling, and the intelligent manner in which reports were prepared and evidence given.

On his return to the Force after the war, he was again commended on 9 February 1920 for:

prompt and courageous action in stopping a runaway horse and wagon.

William Rounsley was promoted three times: to sergeant on 23 November 1922 and to sub-inspector 2 years later on 5 February 1925. On 1 January 1931, he was promoted to inspector and Chief Clerk at Force Headquarters.

As a sub-inspector he was awarded the Exeter City Long Service and Efficiency Medal on 24 October 1929, a local award similar to many such medals of the times. The medal carries the city arms on the obverse with the legend 'for Long Service and Efficiency' and the name of the force on the reverse. It hangs from a white ribbon with two broad green stripes. The medal was replaced in 1951 by the current national medal.

Ewart Claude PEARCE
(Cornwall)

Constable 116 Pearce joined the Cornwall Constabulary after service with the Royal Engineers in the First World War from May 1916 to November 1919 and two years spent with the Port of London Authority Dock Police (19 June 1922 to 31 October 1924). During his war service he won the Military Medal for:

devotion to duty on July 21st, 22nd and 23rd, 1918, in Russia, when he continually drove his Drury Car, bringing up working parties and tools for 60 hours as well as assisting in the fighting.

Towards the latter part of his police career he was lucky to survive an appearance before the Chief Constable on two charges of breach of discipline in circumstances which would normally have attracted dismissal. His personal record gives brief details:

15.1.47   2 charges:-

(1)   using a m/cycle there not being in force a third party risk policy,
(2)   failing to work his beat in accordance with orders.

No.1   Penryn Boro Court on 14.1.47, Fined 5/-,

Licence suspd 12 months.

No.2 Fined £2.
Addtl increment not withdrawn.

Ewart Pearce stayed with the Cornwall Constabulary for 28 years serving in all areas of the county, he retired on pension on 18 April 1953.

John Henry TUCKER
(Cornwall)

Constable 134 Tucker joined the Cornwall Constabulary on 4 January 1915, retiring after a successful career with the rank of inspector (promoted 1 October 1939) on 30 September 1945 at Wadebridge.

He served in many areas of the Force, including such places as Rilla Mill and Stokeclimsland, stations typical of the times but long since closed. A list of villages and hamlets where police officers were once stationed in both Devon and Cornwall never fails to amuse younger officers who find it hard to imagine serving at Black Dog, Hoops or Bishop's Nympton (all Devon stations from the distant past).

PC Tucker was born in Liskeard on 8 November 1895 and worked as a miner before joining the Force at the age of 19. Before his first 12 months of service had been completed he joined the Army - the Devonshire Regiment, No. 16117 - but survived to return to his home force on 1 February 1919.

On 19 February 1917 when he held the rank of corporal he was awarded the Military Medal for bravery in France. The medal was presented by the Mayor of Saltash at a ceremony held on 9 March 1920.

The war left John Tucker with slight deafness and the scars of a gunshot wound to his left buttock but which was described as 'quite sound and giving no trouble' in the medical examination (3 Jan 1919) on his return to the Force.

Francis Henry MINERS
(Cornwall)

Francis Miners was another Cornish officer who enlisted in the Army very early in his police career following the outbreak of war. He was born in Truro on 2 September 1894 and began his police service on 1 December 1914 but left 12 months later on 12 December 1915 to enlist in the Royal Garrison Artillery (No. 12826). He returned to Cornwall on 20 January 1919 to resume his career but resigned 12 years later on 31 August 1931 for reasons which are not recorded.

He served in most areas of the County including Launceston, St Austell, Bodmin and Helston. He resigned from Camborne.

Constable 4 Miners was promoted to the rank of corporal during his war service and won the Military Medal on 18 July 1917 for bravery in the Field.

Albert James Endicott PERRYMAN
(Devon)

Constable 88 Perryman (known as 'Jim') joined the Devon Constabulary a few months after his discharge from the Army at the end of the Great War - on 9 July 1919. He was promoted once, to sergeant, on 1 July 1935, and retired from Lifton with almost 34 years service on 8 August 1953.

He enlisted in the 9th Battalion of the Devonshire Regiment (11037) in 1914 when only 15 (born 12 February 1899) and fought at the Battle of Loos a year later; an action in which his brother, Alfred, was killed. During the Battle of the Somme in 1916 he was badly wounded in heavy fighting but recovered and saw further action at the Third Battle of Ieper (Passchendaele) in 1917 when he won the Distinguished Conduct Medal:

For conspicuous gallantry and devotion to duty in command of a platoon. Although wounded he carried on until the objective was reached and consolidated.

(*London Gazette* 4 March 1918, page 2747)

The DCM is the highest gallantry award possible for a non-commissioned officer apart from the VC. He was 18 years old. Due to the wounds suffered he spent a period as a drill instructor with the Hampshire Regiment until he was demobilised in 1919 and joined the Devon Constabulary.

Jim Perryman was the second of three generations from the same family to serve with the Devon Constabulary covering a period of 90 years. His father, who had the same forenames and who was a native of Throwleigh (b 22 September 1868), joined the Force (Constable 8) on 28 April 1892 and served through to his retirement at Wear Gifford on 31 March 1920. He achieved the rank of merit class constable in April 1905 but was never promoted further.

Jim's son, Reginald James Perryman, the third generation to serve, joined on his nineteenth birthday on 22 June 1941 (PC 428) but left the Force for a period of four years in the Second World War (August 1943 to May 1947) to serve with the RAF. He was discharged with the rank of flying officer. He had a very successful police career, rising to the rank of chief superintendent at the time of

A stretcher party struggle with a wounded man through the deep mud of the battlefield in Flanders.

Alfred William Stratton DCM.

A British solider looks out over the ruins of Ypres, known as 'Wipers' to the troops.

his retirement in June 1982 from the Devon and Cornwall Constabulary at Launceston.

A second son served with the Metropolitan Police from 1948 to 1982 and was awarded the BEM for meritorious service in the Queen's Birthday Honours List in June 1970.

Alfred William STRATTON
(Devon)

Officers returning to their forces after the Armistice often suffered for many years from the debilitating effects of illness and disease contracted while on active service. Alfred Stratton rejoined the Devon Constabulary on 3 February 1919 but spent two short spells on sick leave in the following 18 months suffering from malaria in October 1919 and May 1920. He was able to serve through to a normal retirement on pension, however, on 30 September 1933 at Burlescombe.

He first joined the Force on 28 April 1908 as a man of 23 (born 11 November 1885 in Devonport) but resigned whilst stationed at Paignton to enlist in the Royal Engineers on the last day of 1914.

During his military service he won the Distinguished Conduct Medal with a citation recording his bravery published in the *London Gazette* of 30 March 1916 (page 3443):

58902 Sergeant A W Stratton, 77th Field Company, Royal Engineers

For conspicuous gallantry, notably on one occasion when he accompanied a bombing party of an infantry battalion. When all the bombing party were killed he held up the enemy with bombs until a 'stop' had been made.

Edgar HARE
(Cornwall)

It's very easy to forget that the highest ranking officers in the Constabularies were once young, maybe a little reckless and won medals and decorations for acts of bravery in the service of their country during the Great War. Until the second half of the twentieth century it was quite common for Chief Constables to be drawn directly from the Military with extensive and interesting careers already behind them.

Major Edgar Hare was appointed Chief Constable of the Cornwall Constabulary on 18 April 1935 after a career of 20 years with the Army. He stayed until his retirement at the age of 65 on 29 August 1956.

He joined the British South Africa Police at the age of 22 in January 1913 and served until shortly after the start of the Great War then resigned to join the 2nd Rhodesia Regiment in February 1915. He served with the Regiment until his transfer to the Duke of Cornwall's Light Infantry in October 1917.

He remained with the 'Dukes' for 18 years and only left to take up his appointment as Chief Constable. On 15 October 1918, whilst holding the rank of captain, he was awarded the Military Cross:

During an attack he led his company with the greatest gallantry through the first objective. Although wounded, he remained in command after reaching the final objective, where in spite of heavy machine-gun and rifle fire he consolidated his position exactly on the appointed spot. He showed a very fine example to his men, and kept the headquarters of the battalion well informed of the situation, declining to leave his post until he received definite instructions to do so, when the situation was clear.

(*London Gazette*, 15 October 1918, page 12075)

The Military Cross was introduced in December 1914 for award to officers up to the rank of captain and warrant officers for acts of gallantry. Officers of higher rank than captain were eligible to admission to the Distinguished Service Order. The Cross hangs from a white ribbon with a broad central mauve stripe. More than 37 000 crosses were awarded in the Great War.

Major Hare was recalled to his regiment briefly on 29 January 1940 after the outbreak of the Second World War but was released to return to the Constabulary slightly more than three months later on 4 May.

On 12 October 1953 he was awarded the King's Police and Fire Service Medal for Distinguished Service.

Lyndon Henry MORRIS
(Devon)

Major Morris was Chief Constable of the Devon Constabulary from 2 April 1931 until 7 November 1946 when he died suddenly after an operation. He was born on 20 January 1889 and came into the Police Service after careers in the Army, and as Governor of Dartmoor Prison from 18 August 1923 until his appointment as Chief Constable.

He was a qualified solicitor but chose Military Service at the age of 21 and enlisted in the King's Shropshire Light Infantry on 1 January 1910. He served throughout the War and won the Military Cross in France in September 1918.

First notification of the award to T/Capt (A/Lt Col) Morris was contained in the *London Gazette*, 8 March 1919, with many others and a note that details of the actions leading to them would be published at a later date. Seven months later, on 8 October, the citation appeared:

T. Capt. (A/Maj.) Lyndon Henry Morris, 1st Bn., Shrops. L.I.

He commanded his battalion during the attacks of 18th to 24th Sept. 1918, near Fresnoy, and showed coolness and judgement in dealing with situations. When the attack was held up he went forward, under machine gun and shell fire, to reconnoitre, and by his presence inspired the men with confidence. The battalion eventually not only gained its objective, but also assisted the brigade on its left to reach its objective.
Major Morris was later appointed a Commander of the Most Excellent Order of the British Empire (CBE) and awarded the KPM for Distinguished Service.

Frederick Thomas TARRY
(Exeter City)

Frederick Tarry was appointed Chief Constable of the Exeter City Police on 31 January 1931 and remained in the post for almost 10 years. He first joined the Brighton Police as a constable in 1919 at the end of the Great War and rose rapidly to the rank of inspector - he was 34 years of age with 12 years' service when he moved to Exeter.

On 12 December 1940 he was loaned to Southampton Police due to the ill-health of the Chief Constable there and confirmed in that appointment on 1 October 1941. He ended his police career in 1962 as one of Her Majesty's Inspector of Constabulary.

He was a writer of some note and was runner-up in the King's Police Gold Medal Essay Competition in 1931; he won the Gold Medal the following year. His military career was equally distinguished although he never received a commission, slightly surprising in the light of his achievements after the war, although it was common practice in the early years of the war to offer commissions only to those with public school education. He was decorated for bravery three times, receiving a Mention in Despatches and winning the Military Medal and a Bar.

He was first mentioned in the despatch of Sir Douglas Haig dated 9 April 1917 (Tarry No 4299 Corpl. FT Royal West Kent Regt) published in the *London Gazette* of 25 May 1917 (page 5160) and received his Military Medal three weeks later (18.6.17). The award of the Bar to his MM came in 1919 after the Armistice when he held the rank of serjeant (the alternative spelling of 'sergeant' used by some units of the Army until shortly before the Second World War).

His replacement as Chief Constable in Exeter, Albert Edgar Rowsell, also won the Military Medal [22191 Cpl A E Rowsell DCLI attd Lond R (Whipton) - *London Gazette* 18.6.1917, p 6024] and similarly joined the Police Service, in Exeter, in 1919. He served as the Chief Constable from 1941 to 1958 and was appointed as an Officer of the Order of the British Empire (OBE) for his services during the Blitz on Exeter. He left Exeter on 16 July 1958 to take up the post of Chief Constable in Brighton.

Richard Clifford WEARY
(Cornwall)

It was unusual in the early years of the twentieth century for an officer to transfer between forces - most joined their home force and stayed there, although there were a number of small borough forces existing which tempted a few away.

Richard Weary was a local man, born in Bodmin on 4 February 1888, who stayed in Cornwall when he started his police career on 20 May 1907. After three years, however, he left and moved to the Devonport Borough Police in Plymouth (on 18 June 1910) for personal reasons and continued his career there.

He stayed less than a year before going back to Cornwall on 16 October 1911. After the start of the war he enlisted in the Military Mounted Police (L/Corporal No P/2906) and served for slightly less than three years from Christmas Day 1915 to 6 August 1918. During his police service he received one 'Favourable Record' on 1 May 1912:

for stopping, at great personal risk, a runaway horse, at St. Austell on 9th April.

His military service took him to Salonika, Greece where he was awarded the Meritorious Service Medal, on 3 June 1918, in recognition of valuable services performed in the Balkan campaign.

John William WARD
(Plymouth City)

John Ward joined the County Borough of Devonport Police as Constable 17 on 27 September 1910 with a starting salary of one pound, three shillings and sixpence per week. He retired on pension from Plymouth City on completion of 26 years service on 4 November 1936 with the rank of inspector and an annual pension of £233 6s 8d.

He was suffering from a duodenal ulcer and, in the opinion of the Police Surgeon:

it is reasonable to conclude that the necessary conditions of his police duty have probably caused and certainly retarded recovery from his complaint.

Inspector Ward's police service was interrupted by the First World War and he was awarded the Meritorious Service Medal for distinguished service in the Field at Ieper (*London Gazette* 18 October 1916) as a member of the Military Foot Police (Lance Corporal P/1459).

When he resumed his police career he was commended by the Plymouth Police Court on 4 January 1923 for:

zeal and ability in effecting the arrest of a man charged with soliciting men for immoral purposes.

and twice by his Chief Constable. The first occasion came on 5 February 1924 for the arrest of a man on charges of importuning for immoral purposes and the second on 27 June the same year for:

the manner in which he and PC Palmer got together evidence in a case of habitual prostitution.

William Edwin VENNING
(Plymouth City)

Shortly after the war - in early 1921 - the Chief Constable of Plymouth issued General Order No 517 ordering all officers who had won medals for bravery or

distinguished service to submit reports giving brief details of the circumstances to allow appropriate entries to be made in their personal records.

Constable 196 Venning was one officer affected and gave details of the three occasions when his courage was recognised.

His report was more detailed than most and it illustrates clearly the horrors he had witnessed and give a clear indication of the level of courage displayed while on active service:

Mentioned in Despatches, of Field Marshall Sir J.D.P. French on the 17.2.15 for on the 14th December 1914, whilst serving as a Lance Corpl in the 1st Somerset L.I. volunteered with two men to reconnoitre at night, and prepare a sketch of the German trenches 150 yards away, which had to be done by crawling practically the whole of the distance.

After obtaining the information required and returning back, one of my patrol was shot, and with great difficulty I got him on my back safely to our trenches, where it was found that he had been shot right through the head.

Also on the 19th December 1914, when my Company were ordered to make an attack at 1-30 p.m. on the German trenches all the officers (7 in all) and senior N.C.Os were killed, so I took charge until relieved at 5 a.m. the following morning by a Q.M. Sgt, when we were ordered to retire to our old position, only 80 men left out of the Company.

Military Medal dated London Gazette 11.11.16 whilst at Beaumont Hamel for reconnoitring on several occasions for observing the enemy's machine gun positions for the information of our artillery, also for 'devotion to duty'.

Bar to Military Medal awarded on the 11.6.17 whilst serving as a Sergt in the Military Mounted Police on the night of the 29th May 1917, whilst the Germans were heavily shelling the village of Vlamertinghe, several men of the Artillery were severely wounded, I assisted in getting them to a place of safety.

Also on the night of the 29th May 1917, whilst on mounted patrol duty between Vlamertinghe and Ypres, the Germans heavily shelled the road and set fire to a column of 10 lorries laden with ammunition also the screens at the side of the road, also severely wounding about 20 men, which I assisted in rendering first aid and getting them to a place of safety.

I then galloped back along the road between the burning lorries and screens and turned back all traffic at the rear and diverted it on various branch roads.

William Venning was born in Marazion on 13 July 1888 and spent nine years in the Army with the 2nd Battalion, Somerset Light Infantry before joining the Plymouth Constabulary on 27 March 1914. He was recalled to the Regiment less than six months later at the outbreak of War.

He embarked for France with the 1st Battalion on 21 August 1914 but contracted malaria very early in the campaign and was admitted to hospital a month later, rejoining the battalion in late November. He was promoted to Battalion Provost Sergeant on 13 May 1915 but transferred to the Mounted Military Police (MMP) in early 1916.

He served for the duration and didn't rejoin the Constabulary until 1919. He was at first posted to light duties as a result of injuries to his leg but recovered to serve until his retirement on 27 March 1940 with the rank of sergeant.

He died on 19 March 1964.

John Frank LETTS
(Plymouth City)

Constable 26 Letts joined the City Force on 10 February 1919 after two years' service with the Army in France. He was promoted to sergeant in September 1941 and retired on pension on 11 February 1945 but died at the age of 55 in 1952.

During his police service he was commended once by the Justices, on 25 March 1936, with other officers:

for vigilance and efficiency in the arrest of a man for larceny of a car.

After his retirement he took up the post of Fuel Inspector with the City Fuel Control Department in Plymouth after being recommended for the job by his former Chief Constable in reply to a request from the Department for a suitable candidate to fill the post.

John Letts had been twice decorated in the war for bravery and submitted his report to the Chief Constable in accordance with orders in March 1921.

> *Sir,*
> *I beg to report at your request the circumstances for which I was awarded the Military Medal and bar.*
>
> *The Military Medal:*
>
> *At Gouzeaucourt, France, on the 21st March, 1918, when the Germans were advancing, I volunteered with the sergeant of another Tank Crew, in taking a Tank into action, after the officer and remainder of crew had become casualties.*
>
> *Bar to the Military Medal:*
>
> *Near Amiens, France, on the 8th August, 1918, for coolness and devotion to duty, while driving a Tank in action under heavy machine gun fire.*
>
> > *I am, Sir,*
> > *Your obedient servant,*
> >
> > *John Frank Letts, PC26*
>
> *Supt Davis*
> *B Div*

A more detailed account of the actions leading to the award of the medals is given in the Tank Corps Book of Honour:

> *200921 Pte. LETTS, J. F. 4th Battn   Awarded M.M.*
>
> *For gallantry and devotion to duty at Chapel Hill, south of Gouzeaucourt on March 21, 1918.*
>
> *When all his crew, with the exception of the N.C.O. had become casualties, he went into action with his tank on two occasions. He combined the duties of second and third drivers in addition to instructing the infantrymen who were acting as Lewis gunners how to fire from a tank. Had it not been for this man's assistance and keenness it would not have been possible for the N.C.O. to have taken the tank into action and to have driven off the enemy infantry with casualties.*

Above: *tanks being prepared for action and* (right): *advancing through a wood.*

Five months later he was awarded a Bar to his MM:

> *This man behaved in a most cool and collected manner when in action on the morning of 8 August, 1918. After several casualties had occurred and the officer was firing the gun himself, this man (under the directions of his officer) continued to act as first driver and crew N.C.O., maintaining most accurate direction. After the tank was knocked out near Lemaire Wood he rendered great assistance*

to his officer, though himself wounded by being blown in the air by the explosion of a second shell.

The tanks of the Great War carried a crew of eight - four gunners (a loader and a gunner or two machine gunners on each side) and four to drive it. They were a nightmare to drive and designed basically to move forwards or backwards in a straight line. They could not be turned on the move and such manoeuvres involved the co-operation of all four drivers in conditions where hand signals from one to another were the only possible means of communication.

The engine was sited in the centre of the tank and produced noise, heat and choking fumes in prodigious quantities, making conditions barely tolerable for the crew.

The first driver was seated in the front on the right and controlled the two speed (plus reverse) gearbox, a hand clutch, brake, differential lock and hand throttle. He could make the tank go forwards, backwards or stop. The second driver (and commander) sat at the front left with responsibility for some controls in addition to his command duties. Immediately behind the engine were two further gearboxes, one on each side with an operator each, which were used to control left or right turns.

Each time the tank needed to be turned, it would be stopped and a complex series of actions taken to lock one track and apply power to the other, slewing the tank in the direction wanted - each turn, no matter how slight, needing the same procedure.

John Lett's actions when he won his MM, operating two driver positions, instructing gunners unfamiliar with the weapons in the midst of a battle in conditions of incredible noise, heat and smell, fully deserved the official recognition he received.

Samuel THOMPSON
(Plymouth City)

It was not unusual in the Great War for servicemen to be awarded medals by the other countries caught up in the conflict. This most usually occurred where they were fighting alongside the foreign troops under the command of an officer from the country concerned. An act of bravery, or particularly outstanding devotion to duty, performed by a British soldier would be recognised by the foreign Government in the same way as they would recommend an award to their own troops.

Samuel Thompson was twice decorated, once by the President of the French Republic and once by the King of Italy, with unrestricted permission granted by the King to wear the medals on all occasions.

He later reported the award of the medals to the Chief Constable of Plymouth City:

Sir,

Herewith particulars with reference to War Honours etc:- The General Officer Commanding the 12th Army Corps, French Troops in Italy quoted from Divisional Orders:

Company Sergeant Major Samuel Thompson, 11th Bn 'Sherwood Foresters' :

An example of bravery and devotion. On June 15th 1918, commanded two platoons with firmness against an Austrian attack, thanks to his magnificent example the high standard of his men was maintained. He was a great help to his Company Commander.

Awarded 'French Croix de Guerre with Silver Star.'

For conspicuous gallantry on the night of 9th - 10th October 1918, during a raid on the Austrian trenches, and finally carrying back to his own trenches the body of an Italian Commander who was killed in the enemy trench.

Awarded by the King of Italy : 'The Italian Croce di Guerra'

11359 CSM Samuel Thompson, 11th Bn, Sherwood Foresters.

Samuel Thompson
PC 30

The French Croix de Guerre was established in 1915 to reward individual mention in despatches and was awarded to soldiers and sailors of all ranks, including officers. Officers and men from allied forces who were mentioned in French despatches were also eligible. The ribbon carries an emblem to denote the different class of despatch - in Samuel Thompson's case, the silver star indicates a Divisional Despatch. The Cross hangs from a green ribbon with five narrow red stripes and red edges.

Samuel Thompson was presented with his cross at an Anglo-French parade at Grenezza, Italy, by General Lord Cavan and the Commander-in-Chief of the French Forces. The Prince of Wales was also present.

The Cross occupies a unique place in the military history of one of the West Country army regiments - the 2nd Battalion of the Devonshire Regiment.

Medals are most usually individual issues, given in recognition of acts of gallantry or meritorious or distinguished service in time of war. There are exceptions, however, where an award has been made to groups and, occasionally, places; the most well-known example being the award of the George Cross to the Island of Malta during the Second World War.

In the Great War the suffering of the Belgian town of Ieper was recognised by the award of the Military Cross and the port of Dunkirk was granted the Distinguished Service Cross - a purely naval decoration given to honour the part played in the war and evacuation of the British Army in 1940 by the town and its citizens.

The Croix de Guerre was occasionally awarded to whole units or armies, usually French, but including some American and, more rarely, British units.

The 2nd Battalion of the Devons was the second British unit to be awarded the Cross in 1918 for its heroism at the Battle of the Bois des Buttes (27 May 1918), some 20 miles north-west of Reims, when it stayed a German attack in the face of overwhelming odds. Almost completely surrounded the Battalion held the line long enough for other defenders to re-group and eventually repel the attackers The cost to the Battalion was high - 23 officers and almost half the soldiers were either killed or missing.

An official record of the award was subject of Special Order No 4 of IX Corps, written by Major B. L. Montgomery who later became Field Marshal Lord Montgomery of Alamein, dated 11 July 1918:

A Battery Commander who was on the spot states that at a late hour in the morning he found the Commanding Officer of the Second Devonshire Regiment and a handful of men holding on to the last trench north of the Aisne. They were in a position where they were entirely without hope of help, but were fighting on grimly. The Commanding Officer himself was calmly writing his orders with a storm of HE shell falling round him. His magnificent bearing, dauntless courage and determination to carry on to the end were worthy of the highest admiration. There is no doubt that the Battalion perished en masse. It refused to surrender and fought to the last. The officer commanding the Second Devonshire regiment

(Lt-Col R H Anderson-Moorhead) together with 28 other officers and 552 other ranks, practically the whole Battalion in the area north of the River Aisne, fought it out to the last as ordered - a glorious record.

The award of the Croix de Guerre avec Palme en Bronze is remembered today by the Devon and Dorset Regiment at Mess Dinners when a toast to the French Army is made after the Loyal Toast - an unusual, if not unique custom amongst British Regiments. The Cross was pinned to the Regimental Camp Flag at a ceremonial parade held in France on 5 December 1918. The French citation, signed by the Commander of the French 5th Army, dated 21 August 1918, paid tribute to the great courage displayed by everyone involved:

On 27th May 1918 north of the Aisne at a time when the British trenches were being subjected to fierce attacks the 2nd Bn The Devonshire Regiment repelled successive enemy assaults with gallantry and determination and maintained an unbroken front till an hour later. Inspired by the sang-froid of their gallant commander the few survivors held on to their trenches and fought to the last with an unhesitating obedience to orders. The staunchness of this Battalion permitted the defences south of the Aisne to be organised and their occupation by reinforcements to be completed. Thus the whole Battalion, 28 officers and 552 non-commissioned Officers and men responded with one accord and offered their lives in ungrudging sacrifice to the sacred cause of the Allies.

The Croce di Guerra was awarded by Italy in similar circumstances to the French medal but includes awards for meritorious service in addition to acts of bravery. It carries the legend 'merito di guerra' and hangs from a blue ribbon with two broad white stripes.

Constable 30 Thompson joined the Force on 4 March 1920 at the end of almost nine years military service. He served as a patrol officer and also spent time in the communications and warrants departments. For a period he undertook plain clothes duties and was commended with six other officers (on 1 February 1928) by the Chief Constable for:

the manner in which they raided three brothels and the way they gave their evidence against the defendant who was subsequently convicted and sent to prison.

He received one other commendation in 1927 along with the other officers who made up the contingent sent to Glamorgan during the South Wales coal strike.

Samuel Thompson originally came from Derbyshire (born on 30 December 1891) but stayed in Plymouth after his retirement on 30 June 1946. He died on 22 August 1962 in the city.

Charles Stanley HOOPER
(Exeter City)

Constable 62 Hooper of the Exeter City Police had been discharged from the Army and spent more than a year with the Force before he heard that he had won the Distinguished Conduct Medal at the Bois des Buttes on 27 May 1918.

He was a Devon man, born at Mary Tavy on 29 March 1894, who joined the 2nd Battalion of the Devonshire Regiment at the age of 16, in December 1910, after working as a telegraph messenger in St Marychurch, Torquay. He stayed with the Army throughout the Great War, giving a total of eight years' service (Serjeant 9233), before he was discharged and joined the Force in March 1919 on a salary of 40/- (£2) a week.

On 1 April 1935 he was promoted to sergeant (No 10), seeing out the remaining years of his police service as a station sergeant at the Force Headquarters. He retired with 27 years approved service on 28 March 1946 with an annual pension of £210.13s.9d.

The award of the DCM to Constable Hooper was notified in the *London Gazette* of 30 January 1920 but, unusually for such an award, there was no citation, simply a statement that it had been made, along with several others including other men from the 2nd Battalion of the Devons.

The *Gazette* entry contained a final list of gallantry awards for service during the Great War (with a few exceptions). It recognised the actions of those who were missing, killed in action or taken prisoner, and others whose individual actions came to notice as the detail of battles and engagements became clearer. The war diary of the 2nd Devons covering the period leading up to and after the Bois des Buttes has no more than a dozen lines with very little detail to record one of the Battalion's most heroic episodes which is commemorated as one of the anniversary days of the current Devon and Dorset Regiment.

The precise detail of Charles Hooper's actions is far from clear although some indication of the involvement of 'D' Company can be found. Prior to 27 May, the Battalion were occupying a system of trenches and tunnels immediately behind the front line in and around two small hills which were to become known as the Bois des Buttes. The enemy signalled their intention to attack with an intensive barrage of high explosive and gas shells and moved forward as it stopped.

The Devons emerged from the tunnels to occupy their trenches. Men of 'D' Company found one end of their trench already occupied by the Germans who they attacked with bombs and a bayonet charge, driving them out. The Germans counter-attacked with stick bombs and hand grenades to re-occupy the trench. The trench changed hands three times in a short period with fewer than a dozen men of the Company defending the final German assault which included bombs and machine-gun fire from enemy aircraft.

The odds were overwhelming, forcing the Company to retreat, regroup with the rest of the Battalion and make a further stand. Other units in the area were able to reform as a direct result of the stand of the Devons and succeeded in holding the position.

Charles Hooper was a sergeant of 'D' Company and one of the few survivors. Although it's by no means clear if this was the action that resulted in the award of his DCM, it seems likely that his extraordinary leadership and courage was finally recognised.

Edward James LEE
(Plymouth City)

In the months following the Armistice on 11 November 1918 a large number of awards of many different decorations and medals was notified, including the Meritorious Service Medal 'in recognition of valuable services rendered with the Armies in France and Flanders'.

Edward Lee was a Plymouth City officer away on active service who received the medal for meritorious service with the IV Corps, Third Army - (P/1481 Pte [A/Sjt] Lee E.J. Military Foot Police) - from 21 August to 11 November 1918.

Constable 23 Lee (born 9 May 1888) joined the Devonport Borough Police on 2 January 1912 and served to retirement on 28 August 1940. His career was successful and he was promoted to sergeant in March 1920, and then to inspector eleven years later, on 26 March 1931, and finally to superintendent on 1 July 1936.

Unknown Soldiers

Identifying the holders of awards now more than 80 years old proved to be relatively easy, although problems did occur. Photographs turned up on occasions and were useful but often posed as many questions as they answered. Usually there was no indication as to where they were taken, or when, or why. They showed officers wearing a variety of medal ribbons but unfortunately often of such poor quality that the ribbon could not be easily identified. In other cases the medal or ribbon was recognised but the identity of the officer remained unknown.

The photograph of a group from the Devon Constabulary, taken sometime in the 1920s is unusual in that the officers are wearing their medals, allowing relatively easy identification of some of the awards, but not always of the officers themselves.

One who can be positively identified is Constable Richard Hardy DCM MM (with Bar) standing in the second row from the top, second from the right, easily recognisable by his unique collection of bravery awards. A second holder of the DCM, Alfred Stratton, can be seen in the second row, 3rd left.

Two officers, one standing in the back row and the other in the 2nd row immediately behind the Chief Constable (Captain Vyvyan), wear what could be General Service Medals alongside their Great War trio, although neither has a clasp and positive identification is problematic. Only one officer, however, can be identified, but details of his military service are unknown.

Sydney Gould, the officer in the second row, joined the Barnstaple Borough Police on 21 March 1919 on his discharge from the Army at the age of 25 (Constable No 43). He was appointed on probation for six months at 40/- per week (£2) which increased to 74/- (£3.70) by 1 October 1921 when he became a member of the Devon County Constabulary on the amalgamation of the two forces. He served as PC 340 until his retirement on pension at Kennford on 30 March 1945. We know very little else about him, apart from the fact that he was a North Devon man and a sawyer by trade.

Officers of the Devon Constabulary wearing their medals, c. 1920.

Sidney Gould

James Ford

The Barnstaple Borough Police was one of the many small forces which once existed in Devon. It was formed in 1836 with a strength of three constables under the command of a superintendent John Evans, a local bookseller, paid the sum of 12/- per week, whose duties primarily involved the maintenance of order at the local pubs. When the force was merged with the County Constabulary, the authorised establishment was 15 constables, although it had operated at one below strength for some time - to save money!

Also evident in the photograph are campaign medals worn by a number of officers - two standing in the back row (far left and 3rd left) wear the Queen's South Africa Medal (QSA) - with four and five bars - in addition to the Great War trio, testifying to service in the Boer War before they started their police careers and who were recalled to the Colours in 1914 or later re-enlisted.

The identity of one only is known - PC 203 James Ford (3rd left) who served with the Force from 26 February 1901 and retired on 28 February 1927. He spent 13 months with the Kaffarian Rifles before joining the Force and re-enlisted for service in the Great War on 1 April 1915 until 28 March 1919.

One other wears his QSA (four bars) alone. He could be either PC 328 Reginald Anstey (served 1 October 1902 to 30 September 1929) who spent three years with the 1st Volunteer Battalion of the Devon Rifles, or PC 338 Frank Harry Horn who joined on 1 July 1903 after six years service with the Royal Garrison Artillery (retired 30 June 1929). Very little else is known about either man.

Other medals are on display, including what appears to be the India General Service Medal with one bar, but the identity of the holder is unknown and any stories that he or any of the others had to tell will remain untold.

Records held of the Exeter City Police in the years either side of the Great War are more comprehensive than the two county forces or Plymouth City. The small size of the Force (66 officers of all ranks in 1924) meant that detailed records could be kept in a few small registers and, equally as important, the identification of photographs is far less troublesome. A large, framed collection of individual pictures of each serving officer taken in 1924, with medals proudly displayed, proved to be invaluable, although details of the military careers of the men were scant.

Two officers saw service in the Boer War and wear their QSA and King's South Africa (KSA) Medals alongside those received for service in the Great War. Constable 44 John James Skinner first joined the Force on 9 January 1906 after service with the 2nd Battalion, Devonshire Regiment from October 1899 to May 1905. He enlisted in the Military Mounted Police in early 1917 and served through to August 1919 when he rejoined the Force. He retired on pension on 9 January 1936 after an unexceptional career.

The second officer with military service in South Africa had a more interesting and chequered police career. Constable 54 William Robert Russell (born 29 September 1879 at Exeter) joined the Force initially on 5 February 1906 after eight years with the 12th Lancers (December 1897 to December 1905) - he wears his QSA with five bars testifying to prolonged involvement in the campaigns there. In his first spell of police service he received one commendation by the City Justices for the detection and arrest of a woman for a felony (19.9.1911) but fell foul of the disciplinary code three times for offences which are today considered trivial.

In June 1911 he was reprimanded for 'failing to work his beat properly' and severely reprimanded three years later (August 1914) for 'improper conduct when off duty'. His final offence before he re-enlisted was for 'gossiping' on 29 September 1914 - he was cautioned. All three matters were expunged from his record in 1928. On Christmas Eve 1914 he left the Force to serve with the Military Mounted Police until he rejoined in July 1919. He served to his retirement after 29 years service on 15 October 1935.

Two officers who saw service in the Boer War (far left) John James Skinner and (left) William Robert Russell.

In his second period with the Force he was twice commended, once by the Watch Committee and once by his Chief Constable. On the first occasion (7 June 1923) he was awarded a gratuity of £2.2.0 and highly commended for his conduct at a fire at the Buller's Arms, St Thomas. Five years later the Chief Constable officially recognised his bravery as he assisted in the removal of a badly injured man from scaffolding 45 foot high on 3 October 1928.

Three months before his retirement he had one further brush with the disciplinary code, again for a truly trivial matter by modern standards, when he was fined 10/- for 'Disobedience of orders: On 15th July 1935 did without good and sufficient cause omit to wear his medal ribbons as laid down in General Order No. 46'. The punishment was confirmed by the Watch Committee on 12 September 1935, he resigned the same day, effective from 19 October.

Many police officers who enlisted during the Great War served with the two branches of the Military Police, presumably on account of their civilian occupations. Constable 11 Cecil Joseph Graham joined the MMP on 15 November 1915 after two years police service but returned four years later to resume his career and retired in 1945. During the War he was once Mentioned in Despatches and wears the oakleaf on his Victory Medal - when it was won and in what circumstances is not known.

A second officer who served with the Military Foot Police also wears the oakleaf and a Military Medal but, once more, the circumstances in which he won both awards remains unknown. John Edwin Barrett was a local man, born in Exeter on 15 September 1886, who joined his local force in February 1913 after eight years spent as a railway porter. He served through to retirement 18 months after he was due to leave on reaching the age limit for constables (55 years). At the height of the Blitz, however, when war reserve constables were being recalled, the chances of a regular officer who was otherwise fit being allowed to retire were remote. John Barrett stayed until January 1943 when he was permitted to retire on medical grounds.

His police career had been interrupted during the Great War when he served from 6 November 1916 until 4 September 1919 when he won his MM and MID. After his return to the Force in 1919 he was commended on three occasions by his Chief Constable, the most notable occurring in August 1925 when he

Two officers who served with the Military Police (far right) Cecil Joseph Graham and (right) John Edwin Barrett.

'jumped into a river in full uniform and assisting to save the life of a woman from drowning'.

Other photographs undoubtedly exist of the other forces in being in the region before the series of amalgamations, most likely with officers displaying awards for gallantry and devotion to duty - for the time being, however, they are waiting to be found, and any stories uncovered.

THE SECOND WORLD WAR 1939 – 1945

The Second World War saw many police officers leave their chosen career to serve in the Armed Forces. In the early days they were mainly reservists recalled to the Colours, followed by volunteers for flying duties with the Royal Air Force Volunteer Reserve (RAFVR) and, finally, those conscripted into the various arms of the Services.

The war saw the importance of air power come to the fore in modern warfare in a way not seen in 1914, when the Royal Flying Corps was in its infancy, an importance recognised by the award of Distinguished Flying Crosses and Medals.

Many officers who served returned to their home forces after 1945 to resume their careers displaying medal ribbons to recognise the part they played, their acts of bravery and devotion to duty.

Francis Leslie KARLEY
(Devon)

Frank Karley (PC 525) initially joined the Metropolitan Police on 25 March 1946 after military service with the 3rd Battalion, Coldstream Guards (Guardsman 6398995) from 18 March 1937 to 13 January 1946. He transferred (8 October 1951) to the Devon Constabulary and retired on pension at Newton Abbot on 31 October 1974.

Constable Karley won the Military Medal before the start of the Second World War, during the troubles in Palestine, on 17 November 1938 at an action between Al Khadr and Al Qabu:

He remained standing at the light machine gun in his truck and kept it in action under heavy fire at close range. Later at a road block he again kept his gun in action under very trying circumstances. On both these occasions he undoubtedly prevented many further casualties by keeping the enemy snipers down. He showed the greatest devotion to duty and utter disregard for his own safety.

(*London Gazette*, 14 February, page 1939)

Frank Karley died in Plymouth on 20 December 1996.

William Thomas ROWE
(Plymouth City)

Constable 136 Rowe won the Military Medal in North Africa in 1943 and received it from King George VI at an investiture at Buckingham Palace almost two years later after the war in Europe had ended.

He was a local man, born in the city on 9 July 1911, who joined the Force in December 1931. He served for almost 32 years, retiring on pension on 31 August 1963. Prior to joining the Police Service he spent seven years with the Royal Engineers (31 August 1925 to 19 January 1932) and was a reservist until July 1941.

When war broke out in 1939 he was almost immediately recalled to the Colours (1 December 1939) and served with the Regiment for the duration, rejoining Plymouth City Police in November 1945. His war service had left him with a hearing disability which ruled out patrol duties with the Force, he consequently spent the majority of his time in the Warrant Department where his deafness was less of a handicap.

His personal file records the award of the Military Medal in July 1945, a month before he attended the Investiture at Buckingham Palace with his wife and son Michael:

in recognition of gallant and distinguished services in North Africa, the Military Medal to No. 1867371 Sergeant William Thomas Rowe, Corps of Royal Engineers (Tullibody, Clackmannanshire).

(*London Gazette* 15 June 1943, page 2721)

William Rowe attained the rank of Company Sergeant Major at the end of his military service.

He died at the age of 73 on 8 March 1984 near Totnes.

William Charles TUCKER
(Devon)

William Tucker joined the Police Service after serving with the RAFVR throughout the war from 4 July 1939 to 8 December 1945. He was appointed as Constable 167 on 22 March 1946, serving at Bideford, Washfield and Chulmleigh until he gained his first promotion to sergeant six years later on 1 August 1952. He rose through the ranks until his final promotion to superintendent (first class) on 24 July 1968. He retired on 14 April 1980 at Liskeard.

His RAF career began when he was called-up from the RAFVR in 1939 and sent for training as a wireless operator/air gunner. On completion of his training he spent five months with 114 (Hong Kong) Squadron before a posting to the Middle East (14 Sqn) where he stayed until December the same year.

A thirteen-month period on instructor's duties in Kenya followed before his second spell of active service, again in the Middle East, with 55 Squadron in Martin Baltimore aircraft.

In this time he won the Distinguished Flying Medal for gallantry and devotion to duty in the execution of air operations, the *London Gazette*, dated 23 July 1943, page 3327, recording only brief details that the award had been made to:

755191 Flight Sergeant William Charles Tucker, RAFVR, 55 Squadron.

The citation which was not published was equally brief;-

Flight Sergeant Tucker, now on his second tour of operational duty has taken part in a large number of operational sorties. An efficient and reliable air gunner, he invariably displays courage and determination in the face of the enemy.

He was taken off flying duties in November 1943 after breaking his arm and, on his recovery in the UK at Morecombe, he saw out the war as an instructor in Hereford.

William Tucker was personally presented with his DFM by King George VI at Buckingham Palace on VE Day.

Like so many who served in the War, he never spoke of his flying days, even with his wife Mary, apart from memories of friends he made and the happier times spent with them away from the reality of warfare with the occasional lighter moments: billeting in an orange grove and waking up to a breakfast of freshly squeezed orange juice picked straight from the tree.

Charles James MEDLAND
(Devon)

Charles Medland was born on 24 May 1916 and joined the Devon Constabulary as Constable 450 on 1 August 1937 at the age of 21. He served until his retirement on pension exactly 30 years later on 31 July 1967.

During the war he was released from his police service to the RAFVR from 20 October 1941 until resuming his career on 19 January 1946. He was posted to a heavy bomber squadron (514) based at Waterbeach, Cambridgeshire and flew Lancaster bombers over occupied Europe and Germany. The squadron was a newly formed but ultimately short-lived unit - raised on 1 September 1943 and disbanded after VE Day on 22 August 1945.

In 1944 he was awarded the Distinguished Flying Medal with the citation published on 2 June (*London Gazette*, p2535) recording full details:

1337754 Flight Sergeant Charles James Medland, RAFVR, 514 Squadron:

This airman piloted an aircraft detailed to attack Chambly one night in May, 1944. Soon after leaving the target area the aircraft was struck by machine gun fire from a fighter. The starboard inner engine was so badly damaged that it became completely dislodged from its mountings. In spite of this, Flight Sergeant Medland succeeded in out-manoeuvring the attacker which was finally evaded. The port engine now began to vibrate so violently that it had to be put out of action. Subsequently, the aircraft was attacked on 3 occasions by fighters. In the last of these attacks the bomber became uncontrollable and went into a steep dive. It seemed as if the aircraft would have to be abandoned but Flight Sergeant Medland succeeded in regaining control and afterwards flew the badly damaged aircraft to base. He proved himself to be a skilful, courageous and resolute captain and pilot.

The class structure of the Armed Forces with the distinction between officers, non-commissioned officers (NCOs) and men was reflected in the nature of the award made for identical acts of bravery.

In the Royal Air Force: 'an act or acts of valour, courage, or devotion to duty performed whilst flying in active operations against the enemy,' performed by an officer, was recognised by the award of a decoration - the Distinguished Flying Cross. An identical act performed by an NCO or airman was rewarded with the Distinguished Flying Medal. The ribbons of both awards are similar - diagonal mauve and white stripes - with those of the Cross, at 3 mm, being twice the width of the Medal.

Similar distinctions to rank applied to most awards: the Victoria Cross and Mention in Despatches were the only two military decorations awarded without consideration of the rank of the recipient.

In 1993 a review of gallantry awards was conducted at the instigation of the Prime Minister, John Major, and changes made to the system. The rank of the recipient ceased to have a bearing on the decoration awarded and a number of long-established medals were discontinued, including the Military Medal, Distinguished Conduct Medal and Distinguished Flying Medal. The Crosses formerly awarded only to officers were retained but servicemen and women of all ranks were eligible.

Charles Medland spent the final months of the war as a prisoner of war. Returning from a raid over Germany his aircraft was hit and severely damaged, one wing fell off totally causing it to spiral down 20 000 feet in two minutes - a terrifying ordeal. As it fell it rotated like a sycamore leaf and landed on a railway line. Although severely injured, his life was saved by the skills of the German doctors and nurses - he survived to return to his police career.

Arthur McCARTNEY
(Devon)

Arthur McCartney (born 3 March 1919) came to the Devon Constabulary on 1 July 1962 as an assistant chief constable (ACC) after serving with his native Lancashire Constabulary from 2 July 1938. He was later appointed Deputy Chief Constable (DCC) and retired on the very last day of 1976, staying in his adopted county at Exeter.

In 1970 he was awarded the Queen's Police Medal for Distinguished Service. Mr McCartney was a popular chief officer renowned for his pronounced north-country accent, sense of fun and a refusal to waste words - he is still referred to with some affection by those who knew him - a situation not always true of senior police officers and their subordinates.

He left his police career during the war to volunteer for flying duties with the RAFVR, returning to Lancashire wearing the ribbon of the Distinguished Flying Cross and a silver rose to signify the award of a Bar.

His police career got off to a good start - shortly after joining as a cadet in 1935 he was taken in as a lodger by a kindly lady on a temporary basis. He stayed for three years and later married the lady's niece, Gladys.

After his appointment as a constable he was posted to Wigan and had barely set foot in the town before he made some sort of police history and put himself on the wrong side of his superintendent. On duty, as soon as he arrived, he was dispatched by his sergeant down a long road with instructions to proceed to a distant bridge, all the while displaying an air of masterly inactivity until the sergeant could meet him and properly allocate his duties for that day.

Standing and waiting on the bridge he witnessed a light aircraft crash-land on a nearby ploughed field, luckily with only slight injuries sustained by the pilot. Straight out of training school he was able to remind the sergeant that the pilot should have with him his licence and an airworthiness certificate for the aircraft and was sent to examine both. The injured pilot had neither but offered to produce them the following day once his injuries had been treated.

Young Constable McCartney was told to give the pilot a form to produce them! The sergeant was reminded that these forms were for drivers of motor vehicles to produce their documents under the Road Traffic Act of 1930 with the legislation clearly printed at the top of the form!

Undeterred he told Arthur to strike out the offending words and replace them with 'Air Navigation Order 1936' thereby giving him all the authority he need. This was done and the required documents were duly produced at the appointed police station - his superintendent, however, was far from pleased with this display of initiative.

After the outbreak of war Arthur volunteered for flying duties with the RAFVR and was sent initially to train as an observer at 45 Air School, East London, South Africa. Before the course had been completed the RAF started conversion to four-engined heavy bombers with a need for larger crews with different skills - he transferred to the first air bombers course there and, when qualified, he was posted to 101 Squadron at Ludford Magna. He arrived on the day the squadron returned from the first RAF raid on Peenemünde, home of the V1s and V2s used later to terrorise the UK.

He survived his first tour of operations: 'a few interesting experiences but nothing that stopped us getting our feet back on the ground' and, on 2 June 1944, he was awarded the Distinguished Flying Cross:

Pilot Officer Arthur McCartney (161284) RAFVR No 101 Squadron

Pilot Officer McCartney has completed 25 sorties comprising 169.00 hours with splendid courage and resolution. At all times keen and efficient, he has carried out his duties with a splendid offensive spirit, and his coolness in action contributes to the high standard of morale of the remainder of the Crew.

A period as an instructor with the conversion unit at Blyton, Lincolnshire followed until he returned to operational duties in September 1943 with 166 Squadron at Kirmington.

He completed a second tour of duty with his experience recognised by his position as squadron bombing leader and was awarded a Bar to his DFC in October 1945:

Since the award of the Distinguished Flying Cross, this officer has commenced a second tour of operational duty and has participated in attacks against some of the most heavily defended targets in the Ruhr Valley. As squadron bombing leader he has always displayed cool courage in the face of the enemy while by his fine fighting spirit and cheerful devotion to duty he has set an inspiring example to all. Under the leadership of Flight Lieutenant McCartney the squadron has attained a high standard of bombing accuracy.

(*London Gazette,* 26 October 1945)

166 Squadron suffered heavily during the bombing campaign in the later years of the war - of the 199 aircraft delivered to the squadron, 139 were lost on operational duty over Germany and Occupied Europe and 33 crashed in the UK leaving only 27 for transfer to a training rôle at the end of hostilities in 1945.

In the midst of the horror of war and living with the realisation that their job was dangerous almost beyond imagination light-hearted stories abounded: stories of one colleague who parachuted right into the centre of Nürnberg gaol after being shot down, and a navigator left in his crippled aircraft searching for his parachute as the rest of the crew, including the captain, baled out.

*Arthur McCartney (centre),
Bombing Leader 166 Squadron*

Many aircrew were careless with their parachute pack but usually stowed them within easy reach, often using them as a seat to give some protection to a certain part of their body (others have been known to sit on a steel helmet for the same reason!). The navigator placed his casually beside his table where it stayed safe until the aircraft was hit and forced into a starboard corkscrew downwards. The aircraft's motion sent the pack moving around under the table resisting all the navigator's efforts to lay his hands on it. He was still scrambling around under the table in the midst of utter confusion when the last of the other crew members left the aircraft.

As he sat on the step leading out, with the hatch gone, the aircraft spiralling downwards and certain death facing him he felt a bump in his back, looked around and saw his pack had found him. The navigator gratefully put it on and jumped - he reached the ground safely and without injury, only to fall straight into an anti-aircraft battery where he was relieved of his watch and cigarettes before being taken away to spend the rest of the war as a POW.

Arthur McCartney returned to the Police Service in Lancashire and was posted to Alverston in the Lake District, a quiet spot with barely 16 000 inhabitants, where the only sound heard after 9 pm was the ticking of the bank clock.

A more active life beckoned for the young, ambitious officer which came in the form of a move to the CID at Seaforth, Liverpool - more his cup of tea, and a posting which lead to promotion to sergeant at Ashton-under-Makerfield in due course.

With his potential recognised by his senior officers it was decided that he needed experience of policing in a city environment and was duly sent to Prestwick, Manchester, as a detective sergeant followed with a further spell at Leigh until his promotion to inspector at the Force Training School.

A map of the police forces of the UK in the early 1950s looked very different from today - Manchester had its own force, as did Salford and Liverpool, the rest were policed by the Lancashire County Constabulary - the 'great' amalgamations of the 60s were still some way distant and imaginative new counties glorying in such names as Greater Manchester, Merseyside or the West Midlands were still dreams in the minds of civil servants and bureaucrats.

Further promotions to chief inspector as second-in-command of the Traffic Department (later upgraded to superintendent) and chief superintendent in the Leyland Division followed. When he left Lancashire in 1962 to move to the Devon Constabulary as an ACC he was in charge of the Chorley Division as a chief superintendent.

On his first day with his new force he met up with John Jenkins, then a sergeant in charge of the Force Accident Prevention Unit, and renewed a friendship which was to last until John's death 30 years later.

Martin Clifford WRIGHT
(Plymouth City)

Cliff Wright joined the Plymouth City Police on 8 July 1946, one month after his demob from the RAF. He served for 26 years but stayed with the Devon and Cornwall Constabulary as a member of the support staff. His father (William John Wright) had previously served with City Force (retired 1938) and Cliff was given his father's old collar number - 178 - on joining.

Constable Wright Senior initially applied to join the Devonport Borough Police in 1907 but was turned down on the grounds that he wasn't big enough to serve in the Borough. He succeeded in gaining entry to the Metropolitan Police however and served in London until 1912. Devonport then apparently had a change of heart and gladly took him on to their strength when he applied for a transfer - a fully trained officer of four year's experience being a more attractive proposition.

Cliff Wright had his sights on a police career but his plans were changed by the outbreak of war in 1939 when he was 17. He enlisted in the RAFVR (serial number 1317737) on 24 April 1941 as an AC2 and trained as a navigator in the UK and Canada until his posting to operational duties on 15 July 1943 with 9 Squadron at RAF Bardney as a Flight Sergeant.

Over the following year he flew 30 sorties over heavily defended targets in Germany and occupied Europe including Berlin, Hamburg, Hanover and Kassel with 9 and 44 Squadrons. The danger hardly needs stating - one raid over Kassel on 3 October 1943 led to the death of the mid-upper gunner and the award of the Distinguished Flying Medal to the rear gunner of Cliff's aircraft:

Primary attacked. 2121 hours. 21 000 ft. Identified by green TI's. Bombs dropped in target area. TI's not in sights owing to combat. Good fires seen on leaving target. Combat with F.W. 190 on run up to target resulting in enemy aircraft being destroyed. Mid-upper gunner killed and Lancaster's intercom and oxygen connection from main spar to rear being severed and fuselage damaged.

The rear gunner shot down the fighter but later lost consciousness due to the loss of heating and oxygen to his turret but he survived, however, and returned safely to the UK.

On 16 December 1943 Cliff Wright was transferred to 44 Squadron and himself awarded the Distinguished Flying Medal on 6 June 1944 in recognition of his service after 27 sorties and 176 hours flown on operations. The citation submitted by his group captain gave full detail:

Flight Sergeant Wright has now completed 27 operational sorties, including six attacks on Berlin and many others on Hamburg, Leipzig, Mannheim, Hanover, Kassel and heavily defended areas in Northern and Southern Germany.

Flight Sergeant Wright (centre).

Throughout his tour, his degree of skill as a navigator enabled his captain to successfully hit at and destroy centres of industry important to the enemy.

On one occasion F/Sgt Wright successfully navigated his aircraft to Berlin through most difficult weather conditions and enemy defences in spite of the fact that all his navigational aid became unserviceable soon after take-off. Thus by his coolness and determination to reach the target, he enabled his crew to successfully complete still another operation against the German Capital.

F/Sgt Wright has, throughout his tour exhibited untiring zeal and determination to carry out any mission to which he was assigned and recognition of his work is strongly recommended.

I strongly recommend Flight Sergeant Wright for a Non-Immediate Award of the Distinguished Flying Medal.

Cliff Wright was commissioned in mid 1944 and ended his RAF career as an observer in the two-seat Mosquito aircraft after a further 22 sorties over Germany, including Berlin. He was discharged with the rank of Flying Officer.

He returned to Plymouth and joined his home force, serving his first six years at the Octagon police station with one intervening six month spell as an aide to CID in 1949/50. He was promoted to sergeant on 14 November 1957 at Camels Head after a period in the Chief Constable's office and a further year with the CID. He stayed at Camels Head for seven months before returning to duty in the Chief Constable's office for two more years.

Further promotion to inspector came on 1 April 1962 at Crownhill although he stayed there only a short time until his third, and longest, spell in the Chief's office (four years). After the Plymouth City Police amalgamated with the other forces in the two counties to form the present constabulary he received his final promotion to West Park police station (now closed) until he retired in 1972.

Richard George PITTS
(Devon)

Richard Pitts' police career was interrupted by the war and he returned to the Devon Constabulary having won the Distinguished Flying Cross in 1945 whilst serving with the RAFVR. The *London Gazette* entry gives no details of the circumstances of his actions, simply a statement that the award was made:

Air Ministry, 20th February, 1945

The KING has been graciously pleased to approve the following award:

Distinguished Flying Cross

Richard George PITTS   (183426) RAFVR 102 Sqn.

Constable 289 Pitts was a local man, born in Torquay but raised in Budleigh Salterton, who joined the Devon Constabulary on 1 October 1938 at the age of 21. He served at Newton Abbot until 26 January 1942 when he left to serve with the RAFVR as a flying officer (commissioned in August 1944) - volunteering for flying duties as he had no wish to fight 'in the trenches'.

He resumed his police career on 29 August 1945 at Teignmouth (6 years) and Ivybridge (6 years) before moving to Tedburn St Mary where he retired on pension on 20 October 1963.

During the Blitz on Plymouth in 1941 and 42 with other officers he was sent to the city to help out on several occasions before volunteering for flying duties with the RAF.

He joined 102 (Ceylon) Squadron of 4 Group, Bomber Command and flew a total of 35 missions over France and Germany as the bomb aimer in a Halifax III bomber - lying on his stomach in the very front of the aircraft, trying to ensure that the bombs were dropped on target, with an ever-present very real chance that they would be hit by flak - described by Richard as being so heavy on occasions that he could have walked from one burst to another for miles.

In 24 missions over Germany his aircraft was hit 22 times, usually only superficially but, on 11 September 1944, it sustained damage so severe that the crew were fortunate to survive and return safely to the UK.

The control column was jammed by hits from the anti-aircraft fire, the hydraulics were damaged and the intercom system was destroyed - the chances of completing the flight back to the home base in York seemed remote.

With Richard Pitts and the navigator helping the pilot fly the lumbering, barely controllable aircraft, they succeeded in reaching Sussex where they were able to land at the crash aerodrome of RAF Woodbridge - an airfield specially set aside close to the coast on friendly soil to receive damaged aircraft without the danger of crashing on to operational airfields.

An examination of the damage revealed how close the crew were to a premature end to their flying careers - the control wires to the rear ailerons and control surfaces were damaged and almost, but not quite, cut through, they held together long enough to get home - had they broken, they would have crashed.

The pilot was awarded an immediate DFC for his actions. Richard Pitts and the navigator were awarded the decoration some months later for:

displaying the utmost fortitude, courage and devotion to duty in operations against the enemy.

If aircrew were shot down or forced to bale out over enemy territory, especially Germany itself, their lives were in great danger and capture was an option to be

Richard Pitts (front row, fifth from left), newly qualified

avoided. Each aircraft was supplied with an escape pack containing a number of aids, including a silk map of Europe and banknotes - German, Dutch, Belgian, French, whichever was appropriate. In addition, each member of the crew carried a small compass concealed in the stem of an old pipe, a tunic button or a collar stud. With these they were expected to evade capture and make their way to safety.

In the later stages of the war, as the Red Army advanced from the east, there was the added danger of an encounter with Soviet troops, many of whom would never have seen a British airman and have little or no understanding of English. The escape pack contained a silk document with a few words of Russian, instructions on how to behave, and a Union Flag which they were advised to wear prominently outside the tunic if an encounter was likely. All crew were urged to learn by heart the phrase 'I am English' - reproduced in the Cyrillic alphabet, phonetically and in English, in large clear print.

The bombing raids over Germany presented a clear opportunity to spread propaganda intended to demoralise the German people and, hopefully, hasten the Allied victory which had become inevitable after the invasion of France in June 1944. Bomb-aimers dropped huge numbers of leaflets addressed to German women and mothers, urging them to surrender or to rise up and over-throw Hitler to save their husbands, sons and brothers further suffering in a fight they could no longer win. One leaflet showed a photo of the graves of German soldiers killed in action in a hopeless battle and another of a soldier, no more than a boy, who had been taken prisoner and 'only wanted to come home and hold his mother in his arms again'.

Also dropped on occasions, most frequently after D-Day, were forged food ration cards (*lebensmittelkarte*) described as a gift from the Führer (*Füheregeschenk*) to servicemen on leave from the front (*für Fronturlauber*). The cards entitled the holder to 500 grams of a few basic necessities - wheat flour (*weitzenmehl*), cereal products (*nährmittel*) or beans (*hülsenfrüchte*). The intention

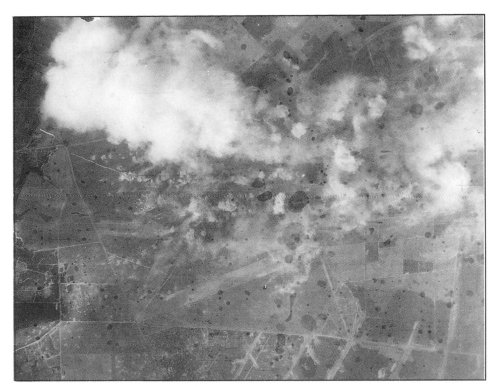

Target photos dated 3 September 1944 (left) and 7 October 1944 (below). They show the effects of a bombload of nine 1000lb and four 500lb bombs.

Nummer 42 | **Luftpost** | Extra-blatt

Deutsche Frauen, deutsche Mütter!

Jetzt ist die Zeit gekommen, wo auch die deutsche Frau dazu beitragen muss, dem sinnlosen Blutvergiessen an den Fronten ein Ende zu bereiten.

Der Krieg ist unwiderruflich verloren. Das wussten auch dank ihrer militärischen Schulung und ihrer genauen Kenntnis der Lage die deutschen Generale. Darum unternahmen sie am 20. Juli einen Putsch, um Deutschland das zu bringen, was es jetzt am nötigsten braucht:

Frieden!

SIE STARBEN AUF DER STRASSE NACH CHERBOURG....

. . . aber Cherbourgs Schicksal war bereits entschieden. Ihr Opfer war umsonst, genau so umsonst wie das Opfer derer, die heute an allen Fronten fallen. Denn auch das Ende des Krieges ist bereits entschieden.

Das wissen auch Hitler und die Partei, die den Frieden nicht wollen, weil Frieden für sie und ihre Helfershelfer das sichere Ende bedeutet. Um ihr eigenes Ende ein paar Wochen hinauszuschieben, darum opfern sie jetzt Eure Männer, Söhne und Brüder.

Schreibt Euren Männern die Wahrheit ins Feld!

Schreibt ihnen, dass jeder, der sich jetzt noch opfert, für eine verlorene Sache fällt.

Schreibt ihnen, dass jeder, der jetzt sinnlos weiterkämpft, nur den verlorenen Krieg verlängert und den Frieden verhindert.

Schreibt ihnen, dass sie jetzt, nachdem die Entscheidung gefallen ist, nur noch eine Pflicht haben : sich Euch und Eurer Familie zu erhalten, um dann mit heilen Gliedern an den Wiederaufbau heranzugehen, der ohnehin schwer genug sein wird.

Schreibt ihnen, bevor es zu spät ist!

ER WIRD ZURÜCKKEHREN
Ihn wird seine Mutter eines Tages wieder in die Arme schliessen können, wenn er aus der Kriegsgefangenschaft heimkehrt. Und dann wird auch er dabei sein, wenn es an den Wiederaufbau geht.

G.26

A propaganda leaflet, front and back (opposite).

So leben deutsche Kriegsgefangene

SO SIEHT DIE LAGERSTRASSE AUS
Die Baracken sind einfach, aber gemütlich. Sie sind wetterfest gebaut. Jede Hütte hat ihren windgeschützten Eingang.

JEDE HÜTTE HAT IHREN GARTEN
Blumenzucht-„Wettbewerbe" sind die grosse Mode.

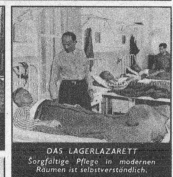

BLICK IN DEN SPEISERAUM
Eigene Küche, eigene Köche sorgen für reichliche und schmackhafte Mahlzeiten.

BEI DER ARBEIT
Die Werkstätten sind mit modernsten Werkzeugmaschinen ausgestattet.

HOLZFÄLLEN IST SEHR BELIEBT
Gefangene können auf Wunsch ausserhalb des Lagers gegen gute Bezahlung in der Forst- und Landwirtschaft beschäftigt werden.

DAS LAGERLAZARETT
Sorgfältige Pflege in modernen Räumen ist selbstverständlich.

FÜR FORTBILDUNG IST AUCH GESORGT
Es gibt Examenskurse für Sprachen, Buchführung, Technik, Handwerk, Kunst und Wissenschaften.

DIE FUSSBALLMANNSCHAFT BEIM TRAINING
Das Rote Kreuz sorgt für Sportkleidung und Sportgeräte aller Art. Erstklassige Leistungen sind an der Tagesordnung. Fussball steht an erster Stelle.

WIE MAN WOHNT UND SCHLÄFT
In den Baracken herrscht grösste Sauberkeit. Alles ist praktisch eingerichtet.

SPAZIERGANG IM FREIEN
Ein Hornsignal lädt zu einem Spaziergang ausserhalb des Stacheldrahtes ein. Eigene Schildwachen haben die Verantwortung, dass alle zurückkehren.

Richard Pitts (3rd right) and crew, with their Halifax III bomber.

was to attempt to subvert the German economy and war planning by throwing the food distribution network into chaos

Richard Pitts completed his full tour of operations - the final mission being a night raid over Germany on the day they had already completed a daytime raid over France, the crew volunteering to fly the mission to complete their tour and take a well-earned rest.

Richard's wife, Elizabeth, herself saw service in the Women's Auxiliary Air Force during the war and was awarded a Mention in Despatches for distinguished service on 1 January 1943 (A/Flight Sergeant J E Owen). After Richard's retirement they ran a pub in Holberton in the South Hams and two newsagents (one in Exeter near the City football ground at St James' Park) before finally settling in Budleigh Salterton.

Edward John JENKINS
(Devon)

Edward John Jenkins retired from the Devon and Cornwall Constabulary on 20 October 1974 with the rank of chief inspector after serving for 27 years. He joined the Devon County Force, as Constable 158, on 21 February 1947 following war service with the RAFVR from 21 November 1940 until 17 December 1946. He was promoted to sergeant on 1 September 1961 and to inspector almost five years later on 14 July 1966. His final promotion to chief inspector came on 11 July 1968.

In 1945, he won the Distinguished Flying Cross - recorded briefly in the *London Gazette* with no citation, simply a statement that the award had been made:

Air Ministry, 25th September, 1945

The KING has been graciously pleased to approve the following award:

Distinguished Flying Cross

Edward John JENKINS (185548) RAFVR 166 Sqn.

The stark facts of his careers with the RAF and Police Service don't do justice to a well-liked and interesting man renowned for his almost total recall of minute detail - Arthur McCartney, his Assistant Chief Constable (later Deputy) in the Constabulary and a colleague from his days with 166 Squadron during the War, referred to this ability in an address at John's funeral:

His storage of data relating to a task in hand was quite outstanding and much used by his respectful colleagues. 'What is the airspeed at which a Lancaster becomes nose heavy and what would you do?' could be the question. You could ask the Wing Commander or Flight Commander but the best way was to ask Jenks. No new pilot went on operations without being told, for example, the Jenkins party trick for likely frozen interior windscreens - a piece of cloth soaked in glycol. His recall capability was also much to the fore in his work as a policeman. An index of vehicle registration numbers or copy of Road Traffic Construction and Use Regulations was not always necessary if John was around to be consulted.

John Jenkins was born in Swansea in 1920 and posted to Dartmouth with his wife, Peggy, and first child when he joined the Constabulary in 1947. Conditions were rather different from today - there was no married accommodation available but the Force wasn't to be deterred and sent him there as a single man. He eventually found a flat where Peggy could join him - with a shared toilet and mice everywhere.

The next posting, to St Giles-in-the-Wood, was no improvement - a three mile walk to Torrington for bread or vegetables, a butcher who opened on Friday morning only and a water supply which operated by a pump in the kitchen. It took 32 pumps to fill a kettle and neighbours were without water until Peggy had pumped it up (her first task of the day). The local policeman and the vicar were the only ones with a flush toilet - a luxury often commented upon by the envious neighbours.

Public transport consisted of one bus a week to Barnstaple and a journey during which the passengers were obliged to get off and walk up any hill as the bus struggled on without them, unable to make it with more than a dozen people on board.

After two years there, John and Peggy were rewarded with three years in the comparatively sophisticated conditions of Torquay (Peggy's home town) where he served as a motor patrol constable. One more spell in the country followed (at Avonwick) with more pumped water and a cess pit guaranteed to overflow into the garden each winter before John returned to motor patrol duties at Honiton.

Six years later he was promoted to the rank of sergeant as the first road safety officer at Force Headquarters in charge of a staff of six officers. He most likely

Flying Officer Jenkins (centre front) and crew with Lancaster PD310, taken at Kirmington in March 1945.

did not miss the experience of the local farmer's pig wandering into his garden to give birth to her piglets where they had to stay for several days until they could be safely returned, at the same time protecting them from the curiosity of his dog.

The life of a police officer's wife in the early years of John's service was very different from today - they weren't allowed to work and were expected to stand-in for their husband when he was out on duty. In their time at Avonwick with the accident blackspot at the bridge nearby, Peggy maintains that she took more accident details than John and was equally proficient in dealing with the every-day, routine police matters that came her way.

John's new road safety work entailed visits to schools to explain to the children the dangers of the roads using a puppet show with figures made by Peggy; a further example of the duties of a policeman's wife. John Jenkins could be the only officer ever to serve with the police forces of the West Country who was sent on a course (in Lancashire) to teach him the skills of ventriloquism as an aid to his duties. Promotion to inspector and a move to Exmouth came in 1966 where he stayed until his retirement.

John's affection for the RAF and enthusiasm for talking of his flying days were soon recognised by his constables, especially during his time at Newton Abbot, as a means of avoiding long cold and sometimes wet hours walking the streets of the town on night duty in the winter. A few comments made after meal breaks in the small hours were guaranteed to lead to another hour or two in the warm and dry listening to his tales including one delivery flight of a York aircraft to India by way of several Middle Eastern and African countries over an extended period - a tale he long-remembered and never tired of telling.

John Jenkins was 19 years old when war broke out and, as it became appar-ent that few men would avoid the call-up to the Armed Forces, he volunteered for training for flying duties with the RAFVR, partly to ensure that he was given some choice and didn't end up in the PBI when conscription was introduced.

He underwent his training in Canada, taking his very first solo flight in a Tiger Moth on 30 July 1941 at 19.45 hours - an event noted in red and underlined in his flying log.

Qualified as a pilot for heavy bombers including Wellingtons, Halifaxes and Lancasters, he found himself first in India followed on his return to England by a posting to Bomber Command, 166 Squadron based at Kirmington, Lincolnshire, now the Humberside Civil Airport, flying Lancaster bombers.

He flew 30 sorties over Germany and was awarded the DFC at the conclusion of his tour of duty:

This officer has completed many successful operations against the enemy in which he has displayed high skill, fortitude and devotion to duty. During this period he completed 30 sorties in 217 flying hours.

(Official citation from Air Ministry)

The recommendation submitted by his Wing Commander in April 1945 was more detailed:

Flying Officer Jenkins has now carried out 30 sorties with this squadron, his attacks including some of the most heavily defended targets in Germany. During his stay with the Squadron he has given a consistent display of skilful airmanship in pressing home his attacks despite the heaviest odds. Several times his aircraft has developed technical trouble which threatened to prevent the completion of an attack but Flying Officer Jenkins has always overcome all difficulties. For his gallant conduct and the unrelenting vigour with which he has carried out any task assigned to him, he is recommended for the award of the Distinguished Flying Cross.

One mission almost ended in disaster when two engines caught fire after they were hit by flak returning from Germany. Despite all his efforts to return safely to England he was forced to land in France with the crew ready to bail out and John within minutes of giving the order to abandon the aircraft. John Jenkins was reported 'missing in action' by the squadron when he failed to return at the proper time and the letter to Peggy had been prepared and was about to be posted when he turned up safe and well that very day.

Apart from the Defence Medal, War Medal and campaign stars (Italy Star, Africa Star, Burma Star etc), the DFC was the most freely given decoration of the Second World War - some 20 000 being awarded. They were awarded for individual acts of outstanding bravery and to reward the courage shown over an extended period - the courage shown by aircrew on a tour of bombing missions over heavily defended targets in Germany .

All aircrew were given constant reminders of the dangers of their task - the squadron operational record books made brief references in their notes of the daily occurrences and sorties flown:

4.12.44. Operations. 24 aircraft were detailed to take part in an attack on 'Karlsruhe'. One of our aircraft failed to return (ME. 318, 'E', F/O Clewley) from this operation, and one aircraft (LM. 176. 'X' F/O Hanna) crashed at Brocklesby Park, Nr. Kirmington, on landing. All crew were killed.

2.1.45. Operations. 27 aircraft were detailed for a night attack on Nürnberg and 25 were primary and 2 missing. For this operation F/Lt Pollock and F/O Burke used aircraft from Killingholme. P/O Buck was hit by flak near Strasbourg and bailed his crew out - all made good landings and returned to this country after a few days, except the rear gunner who was killed presumably struck by the tail plane of the aircraft.

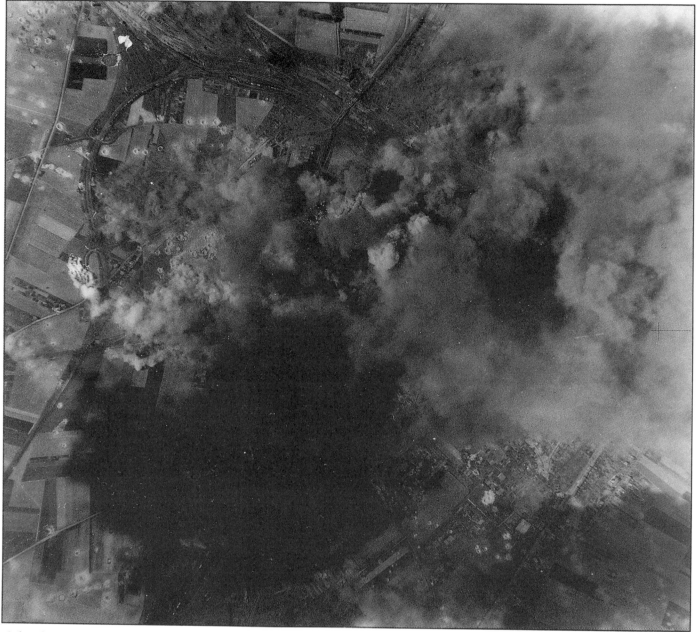

A bomb-aimers view of a raid on Germany in August 1944.

16.3.45. Operations. 26 aircraft took part in an attack on Nürnburg. 3 aircraft - RF. 154 (B), PA. 234 (M), and PB. 153 (J2) failed to return from this operation.

The remaining aircraft returned to base.

Or, in John's own words:

16.3.45 NÜRNBURG. A nasty one !! Losses that night were about 10 per cent. We lost 3 from 26. Some a/c were flying too high over France and should have been below 5000 ft to avoid early warning radar. From south of Frankfurt to the target, night fighters were very active and most of the losses occurred then. I think my nav. logged about 14 or 15 going down.
After the target, we had other aircraft dropping flares to illuminate us for the fighters. We passed under a He111 and tried to discourage him with a burst or two from the rear turret. Tactics of change of course and height (2 descents and 1 fast climb) worked well enough and only about 5 were lost on the way out. Nuremberg was probably one of the hardest targets in Germany and any trip there was expensive.

Lancasters carried a crew of seven - 140 airmen were killed, injured, lost or taken prisoner in a single raid - as far as John knew - there may well have been more.

Conditions at base were primitive : toilets usually frozen, heating inadequate and no hot water available, and this for the officers. Battle orders changed quickly - sleep could be a luxury:

7.3.45. DESSAU - We were called early (I think 5 or 6 am) for a daylight which was later cancelled and we went off late at about 8.30 or 9 pm to Dessau. Home at about 6.30 am.

8.3.45. KASSEL - After about 4 hours sleep we were called for this one at about midday and took off about 5.30 pm. Home about 1.15 am. Everyone was very tired as we had had about 4 hours sleep since early on the 7th and had done about 17 hours flying.

The horror and reality of total war were never far away:

24.3.45. A training flight for the benefit of S/Ldr Laverack's gunners and bomb aimer. S/L Laverack had not had a lot of experience but was Flt Commander of 'A' flight, a nice chap. I mention this flight because on the next day I saw them all die.

25.3.45. HANOVER - daylight. As we approached the target I saw AS-A (S/L Laverack about 400 yds ahead and about 200' lower. I knew he should have been some 2 or 3 minutes behind me as we were to bomb on H hour (or H+ 1). I remember checking our timing with my navigator in case we were late. We were on time.

On the bombing run I saw AS-A hit by a bomb from a higher flying a/c. It hit him just forward of the tail plane and the rear of the fuselage broke off. The tail portion went fluttering away. The rest of it went vertically downwards in a second or so and was spinning very fast. Nobody would have got out with that sort of centrifugal force.

John was wrong, the crew did not all die. Almost by a miracle four survived but were taken prisoner; Squadron Leader Laverack, his rear gunner and wireless operator/air gunner, however, were killed.

Between 1943 and 1945, 921 aircrew of 166 Squadron were killed. Survivors considered themselves lucky and any decorations awarded were well-earned.

John often wondered whether he and his crew were responsible for sinking the German pocket battleship *Admiral Scheer* by accident during a raid on Kiel in April 1945. The ship was not the objective of the sortie and posed little threat at this late stage of the War, there were more important targets:

9.4.45 KIEL. We were on our first trip with our brand new 'R' (PA 321). The raid was aimed at the docks area and we carried 16 x 500 lb and a 'cookie' (4000lb). On the bombing run, the first 6 x 500 lb bombs went off and then the distributor jammed. Bomb aimer re-selected 'single and salvo' and let the rest go in one lot - all 9000 lb. The a/c shot up like a lift !!

On this raid the pocket battleship 'SCHEER' was sunk. Whoever did that had overshot the aiming point by over a mile. I have often wondered if it was our bombs, because that salvo of 9000 lb must have been released many seconds too late. I 'had words' with the bomb aimer afterwards.

John Jenkins maintained his association with the RAF long after he left and joined the Police Service - he was involved with the local Air Training Corps and served as the President of the Exmouth Aircrew Association. He died at the age of 71.

Ronald William RIDLER
(Exeter City)

Constable 70 Ridler served with the Exeter City Police for 19 months before resigning on 6 December 1947. He first joined as a junior clerk at the age of 17 on 20 February 1939 and stayed until he enlisted the RAF on 20 August 1940. He returned to the Force and was appointed as a constable at the end of his war service in May 1946 but, for reasons which are not recorded, he left whilst still a probationer.

The practice of publishing a full citation in the *London Gazette* entry notifying the award of a decoration or medal during the war seemed to vary, with no real pattern apparent. The sheer number of awards sometimes rendered it impractical and the requirements of national security often made it undesirable to include too much detail, but there appears to be no logical reason why one is included and another is not.

In contrast to the award of the DFCs to Richard Pitts and John Jenkins, the supplement to the *London Gazette* for 29 May 1945 gave a very full account of Ronald Ridler's exploits as the pilot of a Liberator bomber which led to his award:

The KING has been graciously pleased to approve the following awards in recognition of gallantry and devotion to duty in the execution of air operations:-

Distinguished Flying Cross

Flying Officer Ronald William RIDLER (169423) RAFVR 547 Sqn.

Flying Officer Ridler has set a fine example of devotion to duty in operations against the enemy. He has completed a large number of sorties and throughout has proved himself to be a resolute and highly efficient captain. One night in March, 1945, he executed a good attack on an enemy minesweeper. A little later, during the same sortie, Flying Officer Ridler pressed home an attack on an enemy naval vessel on which hits were obtained. The successes achieved on this notable sortie were well proved by the excellent photographs obtained. The sterling qualities of this officer have been reflected in the high standard of efficiency shown by his crew.

John Edward EVANS
(Plymouth City)

John Evans' police career was short, lasting from late 1937, when he joined the Birmingham City Police, to December 1945 when he resigned from Plymouth City as a direct result of injuries sustained during his war service away from the Force.

At the age of 18, in 1934, he joined the Welsh Guards (No. 2733787), serving as a private for almost four years. He turned down all prospect of promotion with the Guards, a decision due entirely to regimental policy which demanded that any applicant sign on for seven years, plus five years as a reservist, before being considered - a commitment he was not prepared to make.

He joined the Birmingham City Police in late 1937 and stayed for 18 months before looking elsewhere to continue his career. He preferred to serve in a city force rather than a county and looked towards Plymouth because of its location between the sea and the moor.

He wrote enquiring about the possibility of transferring to the city and was asked in reply three important questions: 'did he play rugby and, if so, what position and at what level?' His answers obviously satisfied the Chief Constable of the day and he started work as Constable 57 in early 1939 at Greenbank.

At the outbreak of war he was recalled to his Regiment but for a period of five days only before resuming his career as a police officer. A second call-up followed a few months later but again, much to his surprise, he was released back to Plymouth on a temporary basis in February 1941.

He stayed for the period of the Blitz before his call-up was put on a permanent basis and he went back again to the Guards in August 1942, this time to stay. He served in Plymouth in many of the worst months of the Blitz, putting out fires, releasing people trapped in bombed buildings, helping the Ambulance Service, placing sandbags on incendiary bombs, releasing trapped horses, driving cars out of burning garages, trying to stay alive - the life of a policeman in the Blitz in Plymouth.

On his return to his Regiment he was offered a commission and, in the tradition of the Guards, this meant a transfer to a different regiment, the South Staffordshire Regiment (No. 292897).

He joined the battle of Normandy some 15 days after D-Day and, on 12 August 1944, at St Benin Ridge by the Orne River led his troops in an action that was to result in the award of the Distinguished Service Order:

War Office, 21st December, 1944
The KING has been graciously pleased to approve the following awards in recognition of gallant and distinguished services in North West Europe:

The Distinguished Service Order

Lieutenant (temporary Captain) John Edward Evans (292897)
The South Staffordshire Regiment (Bath)

(London Gazette, 21 December 1944)

The citation gave more detail of the circumstances:

On 12th August, 1944, 'A' Company and the remnants of 'D' Company of a Battalion on the South Staffordshire Regiment captured their objective on the ST. BENIN ridge. The men were very tired after climbing a precipitous slope through dense undergrowth, followed by confused close quarter fighting. The nature of the country enabled enemy weapons to remain concealed at very short range, and it looked at one time that the Company would be unable to reorganise.

Captain Evans, the second in command of 'A' Company, without any hesitation collected such men as he could, and led them through the wood on the further end of the objective, clearing enemy slit trenches and thus making it possible for the Company to dig in.

Shortly after first light, the enemy counter-attacked and succeeded in retaking part of the objective which was very thinly held. The Company Commander at once ordered No. 7 Platoon to counter-attack. While this Platoon was being brought up, Captain Evans took up a position from which he could fire at the enemy at point blank range. He personally accounted for at least seven of them. He then joined in the counter-attack, led it and was largely responsible for its complete success.

During that day, the Company was subjected to very heavy and accurate artillery and mortar fire, which inflicted serious casualties on the Company. The men who were very tired and had had little to eat, owing to the difficulty of supply, would undoubtedly have lost heart had it not been for the magnificent example set by this officer. He was continually encouraging his men, being amongst them regardless of the enemy fire and doing everything in his power to kill Germans. He even borrowed a sniper's rifle, climbed a tree and shot two Germans who were dug in some 70 yards away from his position, knowing full well that by doing so, he exposed himself to at least four spandau positions all within 150 yards range. The result was that when the enemy counter-attacked for a second time that evening, the Company, now greatly reduced in number, was in a sufficiently high state of morale to beat it off. However, once more it was only the leadership of Captain Evans that made this possible.

The counter-attack had been partially successful when Captain Evans, without hesitation, collected seven men and led them straight at the enemy. This party shot some 20 of the Germans, when Captain Evans, noticing the enemy falter, ordered cease fire and shouted 'KAMARAD'. The remaining 12 enemy at once surrendered.

During the whole action, Captain Evans behaved in the most gallant manner possible. There is no doubt that without his fine leadership and inspiration, the Company after the gruelling time it had had, could not have achieved the success it did. The holding of this feature played a vital part in subsequent operations.

John Evans heard that he had been recommended for the Military Cross and made a note in his diary with the entries for the action:

Friday. 11. In sight of Orne. Took fighting patrol on to important St Benin Ridge. Held by enemy. 'B' Coy establish on new slope. Attack St Benin Ridge. Very successful but reorganisation precarious with 2 Coys L. rear and R. rear (enemy).

Sat . 12. Enemy counterattacked out of mist at 5.30. I counter attack and retake with part of 'L' Coy. Good show.
Another counter attack in evening. Same drill. 41K. 12 wounded. 18 Pris. Coy covered with glory. Recd for M.C.

Sun 12. Held ridge all day. No food or sleep for 3 days but spirit high. Relieved in evening.

In fact his name had been put forward by his commanding officer for the award of the Victoria Cross - he was subsequently awarded the DSO. The long and widespread conflict of the Great War, with the countless acts of courage displayed, had led to a situation where the DSO was awarded where the VC would have been won in previous wars. John Evans was undoubtedly one of those affected by this subtle change of criteria which continued into the Second World War.

In the Armed Forces the nature of the award made is dependent upon the level of gallantry displayed, similar to the criteria applicable to civilians and the award of the George Cross, George Medal and others. The award for an act of the highest level of bravery remains the VC and continues to be awarded without regard to rank. Similarly, at the other end of the scale of courage, the Mention in Despatches is awarded unchanged.

The 'second level of courage' was formerly rewarded with the DSO for officers and the Conspicuous Gallantry Medal (RN or RAF) or Distinguished Conduct Medal (Army) for other ranks. The review in 1993 retained the DSO for officers but it is now awarded for 'leadership' only. The three other awards were discontinued and replaced with the Conspicuous Gallantry Cross (CGC), given without consideration of rank.

Acts of gallantry which are not seen to merit the award of the VC or CGC are rewarded with the long established DSC, MC or DFC, the medals awarded to NCOs and 'Men' having been abolished.

After the Battle of Normandy the 59th Division was disbanded and John Evans, now promoted to Major, found himself with 'B' Company, the 1st/5th Queen's Royal Regiment - the Desert Rats. On 19 January 1945 the Regiment was fighting to liberate the Dutch town of Susteren, a few miles from the

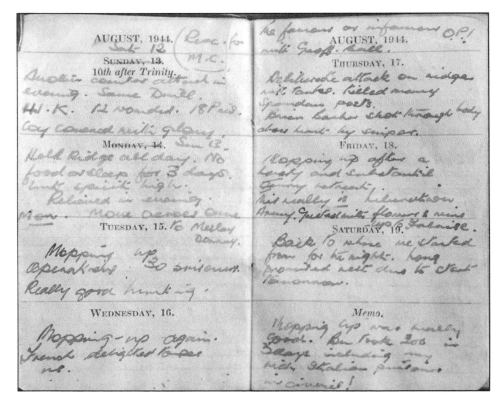

Left: *pages from the wartime diary of John Evans, DSO.*

John Evans, DSO (sitting on jeep), with two of his men in Holland, 1944.

German border, in the face of heavy, almost fanatical, resistance from the German defenders determined to protect their homeland at all costs. The town was eventually taken but with very heavy losses and in the face of strong enemy counter-attacks.

At the end of the battle more than half the Company had been killed or injured and John Evans was left as the sole surviving officer. He had suffered severe wounds which led to the loss of his left arm and finished his army and, ultimately, police careers.

John Evans, DSO.

He was returned to the UK and when he had recovered from his wounds, John Evans returned to the Plymouth City Police to resume his career. His future was, however, severely limited by the loss of his arm with the very best the career could offer being a sergeant in charge of records - a prospect not relished by him or the Force.

He resigned in late December 1945 and built a career first as a marketing director and, latterly, as the Tourism and Public Relations Director in Tenby, West Wales, his wife's home town, until he retired and returned to the South West at Saltash, Cornwall.

John Evans is remembered in the West Country as a rugby player with Plymouth Albion and Plymouth City Police RFCs, chairman of Newton Abbot RFC and a selector for Devon and the South Western Counties. At Susteren he is remembered as the leader of the liberating forces with a school (*Majoor Evansschool*) and a street (*Majoor Evans Laan*) named in his honour.

Kenneth George BACK
(Plymouth City)

Although a delay in the notification of awards was only to be expected during the war years there were occasions when they were almost entirely overlooked. Kenneth Back was one officer who very nearly didn't know that his actions had been recognised - it wasn't until March 1949 that formal notification was received by him and published in the Force General Order No 4/1949, dated March 4:

CONSTABLE MENTIONED IN DESPATCHES

Constable (C.I.D.) 88 BACK has recently been notified by the Under Secretary of State for Air that he received a MENTION IN DESPATCHES FOR DISTINGUISHED SERVICE IN AIR OPERATIONS AGAINST THE ENEMY IN EUROPE, and that this was published in the London Gazette *on January 1, 1946.*

Due to the fact that the constable was released from the Royal Air Force in September, 1945, this award has not been notified to him previously.

Details of Kenneth Back's police career, service in the Armed Forces and experiences in both illustrate the dearth of information currently held in the Force and conceal a lifetime of distinguished service to his country.

Records contain no more than his name, date of birth, height, dates of service and the rank he held when the Devon and Cornwall Constabulary was formed in 1967.

He was born in Bristol on 9 December 1917 and joined the Plymouth City Police on 3 April 1939 after employment in the retail trade. Prior to this, from the age of 16, he served with the Royal Artillery, Territorial Army (152 Light A/A Battery) and was a reservist until December 1941 but not recalled to the Colours at the outbreak of war.

He served in Plymouth as a beat constable in Central Division until he volunteered for flying duties with the RAFVR on 27 October 1941 and left the Force. He trained as a pilot/observer until June 1943 and qualified as a navigator on Wellington and Stirling bombers.

He was posted to 620 Squadron of 3 Group, Bomber Command and took part in several bombing missions over targets in France and Germany and minelaying missions in the Baltic, Friesian Islands and French Atlantic coast.

Late in 1943, 620 Squadron was posted to 38 Group of the Allied Expeditionary Air Force engaged in Special Operations Executive (SOE) tasks taking agents, arms, ammunition and medical supplies to France, Belgium, Holland, Denmark, Norway and the German border areas. The squadron was also involved in the activities of the SAS and took members of the regiment on specific military tasks.

The move almost took place without Ken Back and his crew. On 18 November 1943 their aircraft was badly damaged during a raid on the IG Farben chemical works at Mannheim-Ludwigshaven, losing two engines before they returned to the UK, forcing them to land away from their home base at Chedburgh, Suffolk on the day that the Squadron was moved to 38 Group at Leicester. They were lucky to survive the raid.

A period of extensive training followed the move to Leicester with the main features being far removed from anything he had previously experienced: day and night cross-country navigation at low level, parachute dropping and glider-towing with the Horsa glider in preparation for the special duties which lay ahead for the Squadron.

As the impetus of the war changed in 1944, 620 Squadron played a major rôle in the invasion of Normandy on D-Day, dropping substantial numbers of the Airborne Division troops near Caen before the landings took place and followed this by towing gliders containing more troops into the area. The Squadron also played a significant part in Operation Market Garden at Arnhem, initially dropping paratroopers and towing gliders and later flying a series of missions to drop supplies to the men of the Parachute Regiment and Airlanding Brigades.

The final major contribution to the war came at the crossing of the Rhine on 24 March 1945, the Squadron taking in gliders laden with anti-tank and artillery units in support of the last great airborne operation of the Second World War.

Ken Back received his Mention in Despatches for his navigation skills over a period in connection with these two important events in the final defeat of the enemy. He was discharged from the RAF on 18 August 1945 with the rank of Flight Lieutenant (144609) and applied to rejoin the Plymouth City Police.

On his return to the Force he resumed duty as a beat constable until his appointment as a detective constable on 5 April 1946. He rose steadily through the ranks in the CID, promoted to detective sergeant on 6 October 1952 and detective inspector six years later (6 June 1958).

Two years after his promotion to sergeant he was granted special permission by the Chief Constable to engage in specialist reserve service with the RAFVR, as a member of a joint services unit, training selected officers and aircrew in intelligence techniques. He was promoted to inspector almost immediately on his return to the Police Service.

He was further promoted (to detective superintendent) in January 1964 but, after one year in the rôle, he was appointed Regional Co-ordinator of Crime Squads with the temporary rank of assistant chief constable. His work involved setting up and organising a new command structure for the crime squads with operational units in various parts of South West England and the intelligence structure at the headquarters in Bristol.

Ken Back retired from the Devon and Cornwall Constabulary on 30 April 1970. He was commended six times during his police career by the Chief Constable in Plymouth and was also awarded third prize in the Queen's Police Gold Medal Essay Competition of 1963.

The commendations were given in recognition of his dogged approach to detective work and perseverance, tenacity, thoroughness and ability investigating a range of offences including bigamy, larceny, false pretences, robbery, shopbreaking and safebreaking - some particularly complex and protracted.

On retirement from the Police Service he took up a post with the Army Security Vetting Service at the Royal Military Academy but finally retired to Gloucestershire at the end of December 1978.

Missing in Action

Of the many officers who returned to the Colours at the outbreak of war, volunteered or were called up in later years, most returned safely to resume their careers. Some, like John Evans, had suffered wounds so severe that their careers were cut short - others never returned, their fate not then known, and recorded in their personal records as: 'Missing, presumed killed in action'.

After the war a commission was established to enquire into reports of missing servicemen with a brief to find their bodies, where possible, and ensure that they were buried with appropriate military honours. Some were never found and are remembered on memorials across the world.

Thomas Collins - a native of Chepstow (born 10 May 1916), he joined the Cornwall Constabulary on 1 September 1939 and served at Camborne before joining the RAF (100 Squadron flying Lancasters from RAF Waltham, Lincolnshire) for flying duties two years later on 18 August 1941.

In his short career he once fell foul of the discipline code and was reprimanded for neglect of duty on 1 December 1940. A brief note dated 23/24 August 1943 records his fate:

missing - presumed killed on flying operations.

His personal record notes the payment of a gratuity of £33 15s 9d to his mother. His body was never found but he is commemorated at the Runneymede Memorial in Surrey which records the names of all airmen who were lost but who have no known grave:

The Runneymede Memorial.

Pilot Officer Thomas Collins, 149592, 100 Sqdn, RAFVR, died 24 August 1943 - panel 131.

Donald William Carlyon Hawken first joined the Exeter City Police as a junior clerk in 1938 at the age of 18 years (born 5 September 1920 at Newton Abbot). He was later sworn in as Constable 28 a few months short of his 20th birthday on 1 April 1940.

He left to join the RAF on 10 August 1942 and took up flying duties as a mid-upper gunner in a Lancaster bomber with 166 Squadron, based in Lincolnshire, the same squadron as Arthur McCartney and John Jenkins, although neither knew he was a fellow police officer albeit from a different force.

On 18 March 1944, however, aged only 23, he was reported 'missing', his aircraft failing to return from a raid over Frankfurt. His personal record ends with a short entry of his fate:

Air Ministry on 24th January 1945 notified that Hawken is presumed to have been killed on 19th March 1944 when his aircraft didn't return from an operational sortie. Watch Committee on 15th February 1945 authorised payment of a widow's ordinary pension and child's allowance. (£30 +£10).

It was later found that his aircraft had crashed into the North Sea off the Belgian Coast with no survivors. Donald Hawken's body was however recovered after the war - he is buried in Dunkirk Town Cemetery:

Flying Officer, Air Gunner D W C Hawken, 156366, 166 Sqdn, RAFVR, died 19 March 1944.

Samuel John Richards was a Cornishman, born in Mullion on 15 July 1916, who joined Exeter City Police as Constable 31 on 2 December 1935. He served at Heavitree and Countess Wear until he was given permission by the Watch Committee to volunteer for flying duties with the RAF on 15 May 1941. He left the Force a month later on 14 June. He never returned. The last entry in his record, dated 17 February 1945, reads:

Air Ministry presume death to have occurred while on operational sortie on 13th August 1944. Service Pension payable as from 12th February 1946. Watch Committee on 11th January 1946, approved payment of widow's ordinary pension and child's allowances. (£30 + 3 x £10).

Flight Lieutenant Navigator Richards' body was recovered in Germany and re-buried with full honours in Reichswald Forest War Cemetery (126893, 156 Sqdn, RAFVR)

Frederick Allen (born 7.6.15) joined the Devon Constabulary as Constable 212 on 1 March 1939. Almost four years later (5 July 1943) he resigned from the Force and served as a sergeant (1853859) in the RAFVR with 115 Squadron. His entry in the Force nominal roll ends with a brief entry:

presumed killed on air operations on 19th July 1944, Official notification received on 14.6.1945.

He is buried at Valenciennes (St Roch) Communal Cemetery in Northern France.

Roy Anthony CHILCOTT
(Plymouth City)

Constable 178 Chilcott joined the Plymouth City Police on 31 May 1938, three months before his 21st birthday. He volunteered for flying duties with the Royal Air Force and was called up on 23 February 1942 - AC2 1339904 RAF.

He received a commission in March 1943 and was stationed at RAF Skellingthorpe, Lincoln as a flying officer navigator (139891) in early 1944. On 16 February he failed to return from a mission and was posted as 'missing in action'.

In December the same year (1944) official notice was received by his father from the Casualty Branch of the Air Ministry:

I am commanded by the Air Council to state that in view of the lapse of time and absence of any further news regarding your son, Flying Officer R.A. Chilcott, since the date on which he was reported missing, they must regretfully conclude that he has lost his life, and his death has now been presumed, for official purposes to have occurred on the 16th February 1944.

A year later, in December 1945, after the end of the War, Constable Chilcott was recommended for the award of the Distinguished Flying Cross. The conditions of the Royal Warrant governing the granting of the Cross, however, did not allow for posthumous awards.

This restriction at first resulted in many acts of courage, that came to light in the months and years after VE and VJ Days, going unrecognised in instances where the person concerned had lost his life. The device employed to overcome this difficulty and ensure that the actions were properly recognised was simple and effective - the award was made effective from the day before the recipient died.

The *London Gazette* of 18 December 1945 (page 6207) contained a list published by the Air Ministry of such awards to RAF personnel including:

Flying Officer Roy Anthony Chilcott
(139891) RAFVR, 101 Sqn.
with effect from 15th Feb. 1944.
(since deceased).

This officer has completed, as navigator, many successful missions against the enemy, in the course of which he has invariably displayed high skill, fortitude, and devotion to duty.

The Commission established after the war found Roy Chilcott's body and he now lies in Berlin 1939-1945 War Cemetery.

Killed in Action

The fate of most officers who failed to return from war service is known; their sacrifice recorded on plaques and tablets at Force Headquarters and other stations across the two counties.

One hundred and forty serving officers left the Devon Constabulary to serve with the Armed Forces - most returned safely but nine who didn't are remembered on the plaque in the foyer of the entrance to Force Headquarters at Middlemoor.

Constable 251 Jack Duncombe left the Devon Constabulary on 15 October 1942 after serving for 16 months (joined 1.6.41) to enlist in the Armed Forces as a trooper (14316114) with the Royal Armoured Corps (113th Regiment, 2/5th West Yorks). He was reported killed in action in north-west Europe on 19 July 1944 at the age of 21. He is buried in Ranville War Cemetery, Calvados, Normandy, France.

The Police Service was a reserved occupation in the first few years of the war with only those officers on the reserve list being recalled to the Colours. An exception was made for volunteers for flying duties with the RAF.

IN THE WORLD WAR 1939 · 1945
THE FOLLOWING MEMBERS OF THIS FORCE
GAVE THEIR LIVES FOR THEIR COUNTRY

ALLEN, FREDERICK   MAYNE, KENNETH GEORGE
DUNCOMBE, JACK   MUNTON, GEORGE ROBERT
LEATHERLAND, LESLIE GORDON   SOUTHCOTT, ERNEST ROBERT
LOCK, MAURICE CHARLES   WEBBER, RAPHAEL
WILLIAMS, RONALD GEORGE

"THERE IS BUT ONE TASK FOR ALL – ONE LIFE FOR EACH TO GIVE
WHAT STANDS IF FREEDOM FALL? WHO DIES IF ENGLAND LIVE?"

Commemorative plaque at Middlemoor Police Headquarters.

Constable 463 Leslie Gordon Leatherland resigned from the Devon Constabulary on 4 August 1941 to serve as a sergeant pilot (1316964). He was killed on active service two years later on 25 August 1943 and is buried in Newport (St Woolos) Cemetery in Monmouthshire, Wales.

Two other officers from the same Force left to serve with the RAF and failed to return: Constable 493 Kenneth George Mayne joined the Force on 1 April 1939 but left to join the RAF on 29 June 1942 (Flight Sergeant Pilot 1586747). He was killed in a flying accident after the war in Europe had ended, on 27 June 1945. He is buried in Plymouth Old Cemetery at Pennycomequick.

George Robert Munton (Constable 14) had been a police officer for 6 years when he accepted a commission in the RAF on 1 September 1941 and served as a flying officer (bomber navigator) with 98 Squadron (No 131107). He was killed on active service on 26 September 1944, his death being officially notified on 28 February the following year. He is buried at Jonkerbos War Cemetery in the Netherlands near Nijmegen.

Officers with former service in the Armed Forces were reservists and recalled in the first year of the War.

Raphael Webber had spent three years with the Coldstream Guards (11 November 1929 to 25 November 1932) before he joined the Devon Constabulary as Constable 439 on 1 December 1935. He was mobilised (Staff Sergeant 2654244, Military Provost Staff Corps) on 1 December 1939 and fought for five years until he:

died from injuries received whilst on active service in the Middle East (Palestine) on 15 November 1944.

He lies in the Ramleh War Cemetery, Israel.

Constable 413 Ronald George Williams joined the Constabulary on 1 October 1936 after three years service with the 37th Field Battery of the Royal Artillery. He was mobilised on the same day as Raphael Webber and served as a battery sergeant-major (831976) with 122 Field Regiment RA in the Far Eastern Theatre of War. He was taken prisoner and died in Japanese hands on 11 October 1942. He is buried at Yokohama War Cemetery.

Maurice Charles Lock had 2 years previous military experience with the 4th Battalion of the Devonshire Regiment when he joined the Devon Constabulary on 1 October 1936 but was not mobilised at the outbreak of war.

On 14 September 1943, however, he resigned and served with the 3rd Royal Tank Regiment, Royal Armoured Corps as a lance-corporal (14664958). He was killed in action in north-west Europe a year later on 25 September 1944 and now lies in Oploo (St Anthonis) Roman Catholic Churchyard in the Netherlands.

Constable 488 Ernest Robert Southcott joined the Devon Constabulary at the age of 21 years on 1 June 1938. He was one of the first to enlist in the Armed Forces when the Police Service ceased to be a reserved occupation - Serjeant 143162243, Corps of Military Police. He was killed in action in Germany on 8 April 1946 and buried at Munster Heath War Cemetery.

Officers from Plymouth and Cornwall also left and fought overseas with the various branches of the armed services - three from Plymouth failed to return, including Roy Chilcott. The Cornwall Constabulary also suffered three losses.

Daniel Edwards, a native of Devonport (born 12 January 1918), joined the Cornwall Constabulary (PC 125) on 1 October 1939 and served at Redruth until he was called up in the Territorial Army on 6 August 1942. He was reported killed in action with the 1/4th Battalion, Hampshire Regiment (Corporal 13247740) in Italy on 8 October 1944. He is buried in Assisi War Cemetery. He was 26. His personal file notes the payment of a gratuity of £44 9s 4d to his mother.

Austin Kinver Ware joined the Cornwall Constabulary (PC 158) on 1 July 1937 after a few years spent as a porter with the Great Western Railway. A native of Scorrier, he served at Launceston, St Neot and Bude until 6 August 1942 when he was called up to the Territorial Army. He was killed in action manning a forward observation post whilst serving with the Royal Artillery in France (Lance Bombardier 142475530) two days after D-Day on 8 June 1944. He is buried in Banneville-la-Campagne War Cemetery, six miles east of Caen.

Towards the end of the war the service of officers who stayed with their force was recognised by the award of 'War Service Chevrons' to be worn on uniform tunic sleeves. A maximum of four were awarded and personal files from the Plymouth City Force record the 'award of four war service chevrons' to large numbers of officers. The chevrons were in red and blue and worn inverted on the cuff.

In 1944 a further form of recognition was introduced, on this occasion for officers who had suffered wounds in the service of their Country. These 'Wound Stripes' could be either red or gold and took the form of a small cloth bar also worn on the cuff. Officers were invited to apply for permission to wear them and several were awarded. Although introduced in 1944, officers with service in the Great War were entitled to apply.

Constable 53 Clarence Matthew Smith joined the Plymouth City Police in March 1919 after four years war service. He was promoted once in his career, to sergeant (No 25) on 20 October 1932 and retired on pension in February 1946. He died, aged 70, on 25 October 1965. His police career was unexceptional; he received no commendations and was never defaulted.

His personal record contains a single entry, on 1 July 1944, apart from details of his postings and personal description, when he was awarded 'one red wound stripe'. The report he submitted to the Chief Constable illustrated his eligibility:

Elliot Road Station
B Division

To the Chief Constable
Sir,
I have to report with reference to General Order No 13/1944 re Wound Stripes. In September, 1916, whilst serving in the 1st Batt Coldstream Guards, I was severely wounded by a gun shot wound in the left shoulder whilst engaged in a bayonet charge in the battle of the Somme. The scars are still visible.

I was also slightly wounded in March 1918, whilst serving with the same regiment near Arras, on that occasion I received facial injuries and a number of teeth loosened.

Clarence M Smith
PS 25

Five Years Behind Bars

In the years immediately following the end of the war large numbers of former servicemen joined the Police Service, many with memories which they would largely keep to themselves and which would fade as time passed. Peter Dunsford was one such officer. He joined the Devon Constabulary (Constable 97) on 23 August 1946 and served for precisely 30 years, retiring on pension on 22 August 1976 from the Devon and Cornwall Constabulary.

As a young man of 21, on 13 April 1939, he enlisted in the Royal Engineers (Sapper 2068850) and was sent to France as a member of the British Expeditionary Force, shortly after the outbreak of war, in September the same year. His period of active service was short - he was taken prisoner during the evacuation of the BEF from Dunkirk and 'spent five years behind bars'.

The events in and around the northern French port of Dunkirk in the last few days of May and the first three days of June 1940 have a unique place in the annals of the British Army. The German blitzkrieg had swept through Holland, Belgium and France and occupied Boulogne and Calais on the 23rd and 24th May 1940. The BEF was encircled and cut off at Dunkirk. After a hopeless rearguard action which succeeded in keeping the enemy at bay the decision was made to evacuate the troops by sea.

An armada of 222 Royal Naval ships and 665 assorted other vessels of all shapes and sizes including pleasure yachts, Thames tugs and a London Fire Brigade river-float was sent across the Channel. Between 27 May and the night of 3/4 June 325 000 British troops were taken of the beaches. Losses of ships were light - in the face of constant attack by the Luftwaffe, six destroyers and 24 minor craft were sunk.

Many troops, however, were taken prisoner in the battle before the evacuation or left behind when the Germans over-ran and occupied the town on 4 June - Peter Dunsford was one.

There is a tendency to forget servicemen taken prisoner - we honour the dead each November and war memorials in cities, towns and villages across the country are a constant reminder of the ultimate sacrifice made by some. Those who won awards for bravery are remembered, with their medals and decorations proudly worn and details of their exploits recorded in histories of the three arms of the services and countless other books. Prisoners of war, however, are the unsung heroes and the part they played should never be overlooked.

Peter Dunsford had been sent to France two weeks exactly after war was declared with no training, little equipment and five rounds of ammunition per man. The invasion of the Low Countries and France was inevitable with the date it all started being the only unknown factor. Peter was involved in the preparatory work on the Franco-Belgian border building defensive blockhouses and pillboxes. When the invasion started he was on his way back to the UK for a spell of leave but only made it as far as Dieppe where he was swiftly ordered to turn around and go straight back to his unit. His time in the few weeks it took the Germans to sweep through Holland and Belgium was spent blowing up bridges to slow down the advance into France and it was here that he experienced at first hand the horror, brutality and realities of the total warfare which would become familiar across Europe in the following five years.

The rapid progress of the Wehrmacht caused long streams of refugees to head west across the very bridges that Peter Dunsford and his colleagues were attempting to destroy. Any thought of delay was out of the question, the refugees were unstoppable and gaps in the stream sufficiently long to enable bridges to be blown safely were never likely to appear. Peter saw several groups of people and horses die on the bridges as they were blown up - total warfare.

Peter's unit was eventually ordered to withdraw to Dunkirk where he saw wave after wave of Stuka dive-bombers attack the troops on the beach and the armada waiting to evacuate them; groups of three aircraft, one after another, screaming in to drop their bombload.

He was captured in a small town three miles outside Dunkirk as he waited to join a group of reinforcements. His initial treatment was harsh. As they were marched behind the German lines towards their transport to Germany, Peter was urged to move more quickly on several occasions at the point of a bayonet. Three days and nights followed, crammed into a cattle truck with no food or water, until he reached Stalag 8b. After a short stay he was transferred to another camp deeper into Germany and placed in a working party whose job was to alter the course of a river.

Conditions at the camp were appalling - the prisoners subsisted on daily starvation rations of two loaves and a little potato soup between nine men, rations which were halved when they were not working. Bedding consisted of rough wooden straw covered bunks with two thin blankets each.

The captives very quickly became infested by lice which lived in the linings and seams of their shirts and really made themselves felt as they slept. They were reduced to sleeping two to a bunk, in the nude, huddled together for warmth, lying on one blanket and covered by the other three to obtain some relief from the lice.

Sanitary provisions were atrocious and led, inevitably, to dysentery and a host of other ailments and diseases exacerbated by the poor diet. Two five-gallon drums in one corner of the hut passed for a toilet, drums which were rarely emptied and often overflowed on to the floor. Peter and the other occupants were forced to walk through this filth each time to reach the drums, thankfully fairly infrequently due to the lack of food.

The hut had no washing facilities at all, every few days they were herded like cattle to a nearby river to wash - summer and winter. At the time of his capture Peter had no idea how long he would be incarcerated, or how the war was progressing. For many years it seemed that the Germans would win and his outlook was bleak.

The only heating was provided by a single stove in the middle of the hut around which they would huddle for days on end when work was impossible. Boredom was intense - they would pass the time betting on how high a louse would jump when dropped on to the hot stove. Pubic lice were best and hours passed with grown men selecting particularly large specimens from their groin to drop on to the stove and attempting to measure the height reached!

In 1941 conditions improved beyond measure with the arrival of the first Red Cross parcels and food they had almost forgotten existed. Peter recalls dreaming of his mother's cooking, in particular her suet pudding served with their roast dinners.

His loss of weight had been alarming; he described himself as 'as thin as it was possible to get without dying'. His outlook and chances of survival were bleak until the first parcel arrived. Initially one parcel per week was shared between three, although this improved to one each per week. They contained chocolate, condensed milk, tinned meat, tinned fish and cigarettes.

To men accustomed to very little, very plain food, the thought of meat and fish was irresistible. The contents were thrown in a tin, mixed together and wolfed down - meat, fish, condensed milk together, with most of it brought straight back up. In time, however, weight was gained, health improved and the lice began to disappear as the arrival of the parcels became a regular feature of camp life.

The camp guards were far from the cream of the Wehrmacht and were capable, on occasions, of callousness and cruelty - refusing to hand over the first parcels to the starving men until they had thoroughly cleaned their huts. Peter and the others spent the whole night on the task, clearing away the filth accumulated over many months to present their guards with spick and span, almost gleaming buildings at the morning roll call.

Peter's second move of camp took him to Poland, not far as he later discovered from the concentration and extermination camps at Auschwitz and Birkenau. He recalls his working party being taken to a railway siding to clear snow from the tracks for the arrival of some 'special trains' - many years later, long after he had been liberated and returned to the UK, he realised where he had been and the purpose of the railway track and the trains.

The working party's primary purpose in Poland was timber felling, away from the main prison camp, with the nights spent in barns and sheds close to the forest. At the time he had no idea of the atrocities taking place not many miles away although he did witness one example.

A German Jew had somehow managed to escape from a camp but was captured by Peter's guards and held overnight to be returned to the camp the next day. The man was shackled hand and foot and left outside the barn in the snow and thrown a single frozen turnip to eat. His shackles were very loose and the man so emaciated that he could easily have slipped them off and escaped. Eventually he did just that and began to walk very slowly into the forest - the guards made no attempt to go after him, they just shot him for attempting to escape before he had gone ten yards.

In February 1945 first evidence of the advance of the Allies and the progress of the war was apparent: Russian aircraft seen flying overhead and gunfire clearly heard in the distance. At 1 o'clock one dark morning they were ordered out of bed, told to get dressed and prepare for a march. They contemplated killing the guards and making off to the west but decided against it and began the 'long march'.

Every day for almost three months they were marched westwards until the moment of their freedom. During the march Peter witnessed brutality which still surprised him after everything he had seen and the suffering he had endured.

The British troops were not alone on the march, prisoners of all nationalities were there, including Russians who were in very poor condition. As the march progressed they fell by the wayside and as each one fell he was shot in the head by the guards - in Peter's words, 'they just blew their brains out and carried on walking'.

Freedom came in April. After an overnight stop in a barn they could clearly hear gunfire very close and refused to march when ordered to do so by the guards. Officers were summoned who dictated that the march would start at 11 am or they would be shot. For many days, the prisoners had considered overpowering the guards but had waited until they were sure the Allies were within reach - the time was now right. When 11 o'clock arrived American troops were in sight and the guards were gone. Moments later they were free, many in tears, being given cigarettes, chocolate and all the food they could eat. Arrangements to have them flown out were made but, until the aircraft arrived, they were told by the American officer to go to a nearby, recently captured town, to relax.

For three nights Peter and a friend wallowed in a real bed with a thick down duvet in a house occupied by the German lady and her daughter who were less than pleased to have to play host to them - as if anyone cared. After three days Peter was flown to Reims, de-loused, fitted with new clothing and sent back to England - it was all over.

On their arrival in the UK each man was greeted by a girl from the ATS and escorted to a hall where they were free to eat as much food as they wished - food of all sorts and more than they had seen for five years. Strangely, the presence of the ATS girls inhibited many of the men - left to their own devices they would have eaten every scrap of food there but, even after all they had gone through, they tried to behave with dignity and good manners.

Although Peter suffered no long-term effects from his ordeal he found his first few weeks back home very confusing. Everything had changed and he still had little idea of what had happened in the five years he had been away - he was given a rail pass, a ration book and clothing coupons but didn't know what to do with any of them. After ten weeks leave on double rations he rejoined his unit and was demobbed in early 1946.

In spite of the cruelty and atrocities witnessed by Peter, examples of humane behaviour by his captors existed, even kindness. In general terms his camp guards were 'not too bad' with one in particularly remembered as a 'nice bloke' who tried to treat them fairly.

Medical facilities varied - one particular German doctor in a small town in Poland being very good to any English prisoners brought to him for treatment. He had spent many years in England before the war and retained an affection for the country and its people in spite of the circumstances.

He would always see them first irrespective of the number of locals crowding his surgery and never allowed the guard to be present. He often told them a little about the progress of the war and never sent them away without a sick note valid for at least a few days - days spent in the warm on full rations with no work. He was a popular man who received many visits from 'sick' Englishmen.

Of all Peter's memories, one in particular stands out - a brief moment during the long march west in early 1945. Close to a small town called Eiger, they saw a group of British fighter aircraft fly overhead. The next day they returned and circled the marchers for a short while. The prisoners were concerned that they might be mistaken for Germans and attacked on the next visit which they knew would come.

In preparation they fabricated a Red Cross flag from anything they could find and laid it carefully on the ground as they heard the fighters approach. The pilots flew by twice and returned in formation to execute a victory roll - it reduced grown men to tears and lifted their spirits beyond imagination.

After his discharge, Peter decided on a career in the Police Service and applied to his local force - the Devon Constabulary - for appointment. At the age of 29, however, and in the face of competition from younger applicants, he experienced some difficulty.

His first application was turned down and he tried several other forces with the same result until he was given an offer by the Berkshire Constabulary subject to a medical and his successful completion of the entrance exam. He presented himself at Honiton police station to take the test but was asked by the superintendent why he had chosen a 'foreign' force and why he wasn't joining his own force. He explained and was told to forget Berkshire and try Devon again, eventually being accepted but not without some difficulty and only after initial bitter disappointment.

With 22 other applicants, all younger, he tried again at Middlemoor. Many fell by the wayside or were rejected after their medical examination and Peter was again told that the Chief Constable was unable to offer him an appointment because of his age. He left feeling very bitter and disappointed for the journey back to his home at Honiton.

He recalled walking along Queen Street, Exeter towards the railway station and seeing a young constable, in his brand new uniform, walking towards him and still remembers the feeling of despair. Barely half an hour after he had arrived home he saw a uniformed constable approaching his door and was told that the superintendent was in the car outside and wanted to see him; one man had failed a urine test and Peter was offered an appointment which he gratefully accepted.

The duties of a constable in the late 1940s and early 1950s were many and varied, often including tasks that officers today would simply refuse to perform. The early turn shift started at 5.30 am and was spent cleaning the police station until breakfast at 9 o'clock - cleaning which included lighting the coal fires, dusting, washing the floors and polishing the sergeant's brass pen tray. Police officers were considered house trained and domesticated by some ladies and consequently seen as a good catch.

On the late turn each Saturday the cleaning of the county bike was a job of some importance - woe betide any constable who left it dirty, lacking any equipment, or who had failed to inflate the tyres to the correct pressure by the time the sergeant arrived the following morning.

Peter Dunsford lays claim to being responsible for ending one particularly out-dated practice - the requirement to obtain a leave pass if a constable wanted to be away from his station overnight on his weekly leave day!

When he was stationed in North Devon as a single man Peter lived in digs in common with all other single officers and liked to return to his home at Honiton and stay overnight on his leave. Each time he submitted the appropriate report and got his pass. In time he was 'advised' by his inspector that the superintendent was starting to question the number of passes granted to him and that he should slow them down for a period. Quite why a constable needed a pass to go home on his day off was never satisfactorily explained to him.

Although he had no wish to ignore the inspector's advice he also had no intention of foregoing his visit home on his next day off - unless he was wanted it was unlikely anyone would know - home he went. Of course, this time he was wanted the following morning and found himself before the inspector who demanded to know why he was away without a pass, in direct defiance of an order.

A report explaining himself was demanded for consideration ultimately by the Chief Constable with a view to possible disciplinary action. Fortunately for Peter, Lt Col Ranulph Bacon had recently taken command of the Force and sided with him, agreeing that such passes were a thing of the past and would no longer be necessary - the order was rescinded.

Peter Dunsford served for 30 years at Bideford, Barnstaple, High Bickington (where he met John Jenkins), Ivybridge and Elburton until 1962 when he was moved to the other end of the county at Seaton, staying until his retirement in 1976.

During his time in North Devon Peter met and became firm friends with Stan Pavey and his wife Beryl and was the best man at their wedding. Stan later won recognition for his work during the Lynmouth flood disaster in 1952 and was awarded the British Empire Medal for Gallantry. He died prematurely in 1969 but his wife remarried and moved to Yorkshire for 18 years. When she was widowed for a second time she returned to Plymouth and met up again with Peter in 1990 - they remain good friends after almost 50 years.

A Mystery

In the course of the research into this book great use was made of the records held in the Force museum and a number of medals were found tucked away in a drawer for safekeeping until such time as they could be properly mounted and displayed in police stations across the two counties.

Charles Brown's KPM was there, together with Richard Willis' George Medal and John Lindsey's BEM. There was one other: a Distinguished Service Cross, still in its original box but in poor condition, with no information at all who the holder might have been. There was no accompanying paperwork and the Cross itself carried no name, simply the date of its award on the reverse - 1940. There were no campaign stars, no defence medal and no war medal - nothing - just the Cross.

How it came to be in the museum was a mystery. The inventory of material brought down from the museum's previous home at Force Headquarters, Middlemoor was incomplete and of no use - initial enquiries there yielding nothing of interest. Records and personal files were examined, retired officers who had served during the war and after were seen, spoken to or sent letters.

The local branches of the National Association of Retired Police Officers (NARPO) were contacted to see if anyone could throw any light on the Cross and the recipient - without success.

First thoughts concentrated on the Plymouth City Police and the idea that the relationship of the city with the Royal Navy could be important. When that avenue of enquiry proved to be fruitless, enquiries turned to officers from the two county forces in being at the time and, to a lesser extent, the Exeter City Police - all without any joy.

A number of assumptions were made and a number of facts were known. If the recipient was a police officer, he was a former Royal Navy (or Royal Marine or Merchant Navy) officer, a reservist when war broke out who was recalled in 1939. Alternatively he joined the Police Service as a brand new recruit after 1945. In the early years of the war the Police Service was a reserved occupation and officers were only released to volunteer for flying duties with the RAF. This restriction was not lifted until after 1940 - he could not have been called up.

It was assumed that he was deceased. It was not unusual for relatives of officers to pass medals to the Force after their death, possibly this was how it came to be in possession of the Force although the truth may never be known.

The date of the award provided the only positive clue - supplements to the *London Gazette* gave a complete list of all recipients of the DSC in 1940 - 451 possibilities, surely it would be a relatively simple task to match those names against records of former officers. Far from it: records were incomplete and there was no guarantee that the recipient was a police officer or that he had stayed with any of the forces for any length of time. He could have been a member of the civilian support staff, a traffic warden maybe, possibly a special constable or he could have transferred to the South West from another force and the Cross donated to the police force of his adopted county by a relative when he died. He could have moved here as a pensioner - possibilities were many.

A press release was circulated to the media in Devon and Cornwall and published in the local papers, a television interview was broadcast and local radio stations appealed for help on the Force's behalf. A letter was published in *Navy News*, maybe a former naval officer could help. The mystery, however, remains unsolved. The Force has the Cross in safekeeping but the recipient stays unknown - it will most likely, unfortunately, forever remain a mystery.

ROLL OF HONOUR

Awards, Decorations, Orders, Medals and Honours

British Empire Medal for Gallantry

Commander of the British Empire

Croce di Guerra (Italy)

Croix de Guerre (France)

Distinguished Flying Cross

Distinguished Flying Medal

Distinguished Service Cross

Distinguished Service Order

Empire Gallantry Medal

Exeter City Police Medal

George Cross

George Medal

King's Commendation for Brave Conduct

King's Police and Fire Service Medal

King's Police Medal

Medal of St George (Russia)

Member of the British Empire

Mention in Despatches

Meritorious Service Medal

Military Cross

Military Medal

Officer of the British Empire

Plymouth City Police Medal

Queen's Commendation for Brave Conduct

Queen's Police Medal

Cornwall Constabulary

G E Appleton
S T Bishop
F J Bray
W J Brooking
C P Cole
T Collins
A E Davies

D Edwards
W G E Edwards
W Gray
E Hare
R J Hawkins
L J S Jones
H J Luke

F H Miners
H Osborn
E C Pearce
B R Pearn
S C Rowe
W J Sloman
S Tom

Devon Constabulary

F Allen
W Berry
B Bridge
A J Brown
C Y Brown
J Duncombe
F T Dunscombe
J H Earle
W H Ford
W Gordon
S Gould
F G Greenslade
R S Hardy

D R A Harper
J Hawkins
S J Hosgood
E J Jenkins
F L Karley
L G Leatherland
M C Lock
A McCartney
K G Mayne
C J Medland
G A M Miners
L H Morris
S H J Pavey

A J E Perryman
R G Pitts
G Sanders
S F Sharp
E R Southcott
L S Sparkes
A W Stratton
C E Trott
W C Tucker
R Underwood
J S Warren
R Webber
R G Williams

Devon and Cornwall Constabulary

M P Broome
C J Edwards
R W Goldsworthy
E F Jones

M Kivell
J A G Robb
H L Rogers
J S Shepherd

D A Smith
R J Sweet
L H Thornton

Devon and Exeter Constabulary

G J Llewellyn-Rees

Exeter City Police

J E Barrett	D W C Hawkens	W Rounsley
W J Clarke	C S Hooper	F T Tarry
P Ellis	S J Richards	R T J Townhill
E Fraser	R W Ridler	R C Weary
W Hammond	A W Riggs	

First Police Reserve (Plymouth)

W J Cheek

Plymouth City Police

K G Back	W T Hill	G H Shapter
H W D Beswick	J P Hingston	C M Smith
W J Brooks	A W Larson	F S Stanley
R A Chilcott	E J Lee	C Stroud
V C Cobley	J F Letts	S Thompson
D Crutchley	W J Loram	W E Venning
R J S Eakers	J F W Lindsey	S M Vibart
J Emerson	W C Marshall	L Vicary
J E Evans	F Naughton	K J Walters
B Farthing	T A O'Connor	J W Ward
A B Hawkins	J F C Peace	R J S Willis
A J T Hill	W T Rowe	M C Wright

Somerset Constabulary

J C Hutchings

Special Constabulary

F J Balsom	F J Cox	H Luxton
S F Chetham	A H Dearing	F G Pearse
C C Cooper	P T Gollop	G H Strathon

War Reserve Police (Exeter)

V W Hutchings

INDEX